# THE RIGHT ALTITUDE

**What Nobody Tells You About Being a Leader**

---

Based on 30 years of leadership experience
and 6,000+ hours of executive coaching
with 1,000+ leaders

**DON EASH**

THE RIGHT ALTITUDE: What Nobody Tells You About Being A Leader



The stories and examples in this book are drawn from the author's experience coaching more than 1,000 leaders across multiple industries. All client stories are composites — details including names, industries, titles, and circumstances have been changed, combined, or fictionalized to protect confidentiality. Any resemblance to specific individuals is coincidental.

Published by Don Eash Press
Gettysburg, Pennsylvania
therightaltitudebook.com

Library of Congress Control Number: 2026909385

ISBN 979-8-9949487-0-5 (paperback)
ISBN 979-8-9949487-1-2 (ebook)
ISBN 979-8-9949487-2-9 (audiobook)

Printed in the United States of America

First Edition

Editing by Marcey Beach and Ginny Haddock

# ENDORSEMENTS

*"I reached the CIO role in part because Don Eash asked me the right hard questions at the right moments — first as my leader, then as my coach. The Right Altitude is those questions in book form. For any leader wondering why the higher they climb the harder it gets, Don has the answer. And unlike most leadership books, he also has the practical tools to do something about it."*

— **Paulette Haedo**, Chief Information Officer, Azamara

*"The Right Altitude puts language to something Don taught me long ago: that the skills that build your career are not always the ones that will sustain it. Don has sat in the rooms his clients are sitting in. That lived experience — across 30 years in executive leadership and thousands of hours coaching leaders at every level — is what makes this book different. It's not theory. It's field-tested wisdom I've seen in action."*

— **Scott Lobaugh**, Executive Vice President, Admissions, SSA Group

*"The Right Altitude is a masterclass in modern leadership. Having worked with Don for nearly eight months during a pivotal transition in my career, I experienced firsthand his ability to gently and persistently dismantle the mindsets that limit our potential. This book perfectly captures his transformative approach to overcoming imposter syndrome and burnout, offering a clear roadmap for any leader looking to operate at their highest level."*

— **Blessing Nnachi**, Consulting Delivery Leader, Google Cloud Consulting

*"Don Eash has a rare ability to cut through the noise and get to what actually matters. The Right Altitude captures that — real patterns, real tools, and the kind of honest perspective that changes how you lead. I wish I'd had this book years ago."*

— **Han Lange**, Sr. Director of Global Supply Chain & Contract Manufacturing, Shockwave Medical

*"Don's book came to me at exactly the right point in my career. As I shift from being a doer to leading others, this book has helped me rethink how I delegate, build trust, and develop my team. It's simple, practical, and incredibly relatable — I saw my own challenges reflected in every chapter. The concept of 'listening to develop, not just to fix' alone has already changed how I lead. If you're ready to elevate your leadership and keep climbing, this book is a must-read."*

— **Matt Hoenstine**, Director of Product Development, Universal Destinations & Experiences

*"Don has a rare gift, and this book brings it to life. Drawing on decades of experience, he shares the scenarios and patterns he has seen again and again. With both courage and compassion, he holds up the mirror to help us see how we're really showing up, then hands us the practical tools to build on what's working and change what isn't."*

— **Cristin Hernandez**, Independent Consultant, Product Delivery & Operations

*"Having been coached by Don Eash for over two years, I can say The Right Altitude delivers the same clarity, depth, and disciplined thinking that defines his coaching. He cuts through the noise, brings hidden leadership challenges into focus, and turns them into practical next steps you can apply immediately. Those serious about stepping into higher levels of leadership will find his guidance both genuinely grounded and refreshingly useful."*

— **Adam Shreve**, Director of Research, Seed of Life Labs

*"Don's years of experience as a leader and coach shine through. He doesn't just take a problem or conversation at face value, but completely turns it on its head to evaluate all angles to help support not only immediate understanding and next steps, but a holistic learning and resolution to what might be happening for his coachee. These insights and lessons are invaluable!"*

— **Ashley Paczolt**, Senior Technology Leader

# CONTENTS

*This book belongs to two groups of people.*

*The first are the ones who believed in me before I'd earned it — who extended trust, opened doors, and bet on potential they couldn't yet prove. I have tried to honor that every day.*

*The second are the ones I struggled with — the difficult managers, the hard rooms, the relationships that cost me something. I didn't know it at the time, but you were some of my best teachers. This book exists in part because of what I learned in those moments.*

***To both groups: thank you.***

# INTRODUCTION
# WHY THIS BOOK EXISTS

*And what it won't do for you*

---

This book started with a pattern.

Over the course of 30 years in leadership — and the last seven spent coaching more than a thousand professionals through over six thousand hours of one-on-one sessions — I've noticed something. Whether it was Directors, VPs, GMs, or senior individual contributors. People at technology companies, healthcare organizations, or retail chains and financial services firms. People in their first leadership role or people running organizations of 100s. People who were thriving by every external metric or people who were quietly drowning.

No matter who they were, what industry they worked in, or what level they'd reached, they kept bumping into the same set of problems.

More leaders struggle after a transition than anyone in the organization wants to admit. Not because they lack capability — because nobody prepared them for what actually changes when the altitude shifts.

Not technical problems. Not skills gaps. Not things you can solve with a certification or a training program. They were bumping into the invisible challenges of professional life at altitude — the ones nobody teaches you about, the ones that don't show up on any competency model, the ones that only become visible once you're already struggling with them.

Problems like: How do I stop doing the work and start leading the people who do it? Why do I feel like a fraud despite years of evidence that I'm good at this? How do I have the conversation I've been avoiding for three months? How do I make my work visible without becoming the political operator I despise? How do I know when it's time to leave?

These questions came up in session after session, client after client. Different names. Different industries. Different specifics. Same underlying struggles. And I realized that the coaching conversations I was having individually were conversations that thousands of professionals needed access to but would never have.

That's why this book exists. It's an attempt to distill what I've learned from those thousands of hours into something that can reach beyond a one-on-one conversation.

There are good books about leadership habits and behavioral change. This isn't one of them. This book is about something that happens before the habits matter — the altitude at which you're operating and whether your identity has caught up to the level you've reached.

But I want to be honest about something before we go further: this book almost didn't get written. Not because the material wasn't there — it was overflowing. But because coaching is intimate, and translating intimate conversations into a public format felt like a risk. Every client who trusted me with their doubts, their failures, their private moments of "I don't know what I'm doing" — they trusted me in a room with a closed door. Putting that on a page felt like a different kind of contract.

So let me explain how I handled that. Every character in this book is fictional. Every single one. They are composites — blends of three, sometimes four real clients whose situations and industries and personal details have been remixed until no individual is recognizable. The man in Chapter 1 is really three people from three different industries. The woman in Chapter 5 is a combination of four clients across two continents. The details are invented. The patterns are real. The coaching moments — the exact questions asked, the exact resistance encountered, the exact breakthroughs that followed — are drawn directly from real life.

I did this because the patterns matter more than the people. And the patterns are universal enough that you'll recognize yourself in characters who share nothing else with your life. That's the strange power of these challenges: they don't care about your industry, your title, or your geography. They show up everywhere.

## WHAT I MEAN BY ALTITUDE

The central metaphor of this book is altitude. It's how I talk about the level at which you're operating as a leader — not your title, not your org chart position, but the actual altitude of your thinking, your decisions, and your attention.

When you're operating below your altitude, you're doing work that someone on your team should be doing. You're in the weeds, solving problems that aren't yours, attending meetings that don't need you. It feels productive. It's not.

When you're operating at your altitude, you're doing the work your role actually requires. Strategic decisions. People development. Cross-functional leadership. The hard, ambiguous stuff that only you can do.

When you're operating above your altitude, you're trying to do your boss's job. Overstepping. Making decisions that aren't yours to make.

These are all different problems, but they are all still altitude problems. Most professionals I work with are operating below their altitude most of the time. Not because they're incompetent — because they're comfortable there. The work below your altitude is familiar. It's where your expertise lives. It's where you built the reputation that got you promoted. And letting go of it feels like letting go of the thing that makes you valuable.

Every promotion is an expert-to-beginner transition. You go from being the best at the old job to being a novice at the new one. And most people respond to that discomfort by retreating to what they know — which means going back down to the altitude they just got promoted out of.

I've watched this happen 100s of times. A brilliant individual contributor gets promoted to manager and keeps doing individual contributor work. A sharp manager becomes a director and keeps managing the same three people instead of leading the organization. A director becomes a VP and keeps attending the operational meetings that are no longer her job. Each one is clinging to the altitude where they felt competent.

And here's the thing nobody tells you: that feeling of uncertainty doesn't go away. Not after six months, not after a year. It just becomes a different kind of uncertainty at a higher altitude. The leaders who thrive aren't the ones who eliminated the discomfort. They're the ones who learned to operate within it.

This book is about the three forces that complicate everything at altitude: self-interest, ego, and competition. There are others — fear, insecurity, organizational inertia — but these three are the ones I see most consistently, across industries and levels, shaping the dynamics that leaders navigate every day. These three things — in yourself, in your peers, in your leaders — are consistently underestimated by professionals at every level. They shape decisions, they drive behavior, they create the organizational dynamics that everyone experiences but few people name. You'll see them referenced throughout this book, not as villains to defeat but as realities to calibrate against. Understanding these forces doesn't make you cynical. It makes you prepared.

This book is about finding the right altitude and leading from there.

## HOW TO USE THIS BOOK

The book is organized in four parts, moving from the inside out:

Part I covers the personal challenges of leadership — the altitude problem, imposter syndrome, the stories you tell yourself, and the trap of staying indispensable.

Part II focuses on the people side — having difficult conversations and developing people without doing their job for them.

Part III addresses the broader system — managing up, executive presence, and navigating organizational change.

Part IV zooms out to career and life — when to stay and when to go, avoiding burnout, and defining what "good" looks like on your own terms.

Each chapter follows the same structure: The Pattern (what I see happening), The Reframe (how to think about it differently), The Framework (practical tools), The Experiment (something to try this week), and The Mirror (hard questions for honest self-reflection). You can read straight through or jump to whichever chapter describes your current struggle. The chapters are designed to stand on their own.

Underneath all 12 chapters is a model I've been refining for years. I call it the Influence Framework. It has seven dimensions — Self-Management, Executive Presence, Results, Communication, Credibility, Relationships, and Visibility — arranged in a circle, not a hierarchy. Each one connects to every other one. None is more important than any other, but they're interdependent: when one weakens, the others feel it.

The framework operates inside a container — the tension between two forces every leader navigates. On one side, Organizational Preferences: their priorities, their language, how decisions get made. On the other, Personal Identity: your values, your strengths, your style. Influence lives at the intersection — how you take who you are and make it work inside the system you're in, without losing yourself in the process. You'll see these dimensions surface throughout the book, even when I don't name them directly. The altitude problem is really a Self-Management and Results question. The dentist trap is about Credibility and Visibility. The conversations you're avoiding sit at the intersection of Communication and Relationships. Once you see the framework, you'll see it everywhere.

One request: don't skip The Mirror sections. They're the most important part of each chapter. The frameworks are useful, and the stories are illustrative. But the questions at the end are where the actual work happens. Sit with them. Write your answers down. Come back to them in a month and see what's changed.

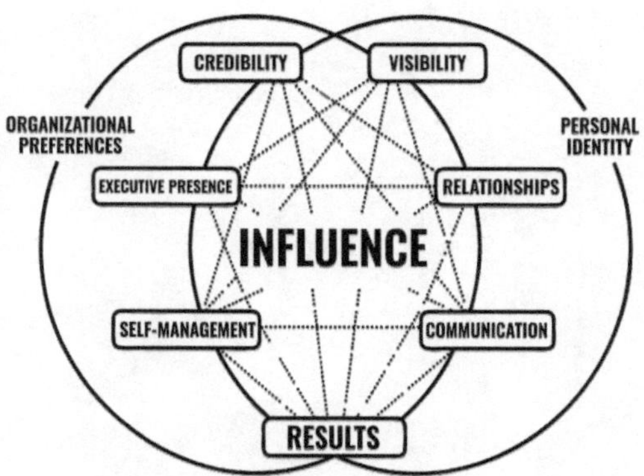


**THE INFLUENCE FRAMEWORK**

*Seven dimensions. One system.*

The answers are already inside you. This book just asks the questions.

Let's get started.

# PART 1

# THE INNER GAME

*Understanding the Operating System You're Running On*

---

*Before you can lead anyone else, you need to understand the patterns driving your own behavior. The single biggest shift in coaching isn't a new strategy or a new skill. It's a shift in self-awareness. Part I makes the invisible visible: the altitude you're operating at, the imposter you've normalized, the stories you're mistaking for truth, and the expertise that's become a cage.*

# CHAPTER ONE

# THE ALTITUDE PROBLEM

*Why the thing that got you here is now the thing holding you back*

---

*"I'm working harder than I've ever worked, and somehow I feel like I'm making less impact than when I was two levels below this."*

**— A senior leader, four months into a VP role**

## THE PATTERN

Here's a story I've heard some version of probably 100 times.

A person gets promoted. They're talented. They've earned it. They were the one who always came through, who got things done, who understood the details better than anyone else in the room. And because of all of that, someone said, "Hey, you should be running this thing."

So now they're running the thing. And they're doing what's always worked for them – rolling up their sleeves, getting into the details, making sure nothing falls through the cracks. They're the first one in and the last one out. They know every project, every deadline, every problem. They're still the person who comes through.

And it's killing them.

Their calendar is packed. Their team waits for them to weigh in on everything because they always have. They're answering questions their team should be answering. They're in meetings they don't need to be in, reviewing work they don't need to review, and worrying about details that – at their level – shouldn't be on their radar.

When I ask them what's going on, they usually say something like, "I just can't seem to get ahead of it." Or, "I feel like I'm doing everyone else's job and mine." Or – and this is the one that gets me – "I feel like a fraud because I'm working harder than I've ever worked and somehow producing less."

Sound familiar?

You'll find that I like analogies. Here's one I come back to constantly. Think of it like steps on a ladder. When you're at the bottom, first starting out, you do all these things. You learn the technical skills, you build your credibility, you become the person people go to. Then you go up a step, and there are new things you're expected to do, so you add more things to the pile. But you don't let go of any of the things — or enough of the things — from before.

And then every step up, there's all this stuff you're doing that frankly doesn't belong at your current level. But it's comfortable. You're good at it. And nobody is telling you to stop because the work is still getting done. So you keep carrying it. Step after step after step. Until one day you realize you're hauling 100 pounds of work that belongs two or three levels below you, and you barely have the energy left to do the job you were actually promoted to do.

**THE LADDER**

*The heroism that becomes the ceiling.*

I call this the altitude problem. And I see it in nearly every person I work with, regardless of their industry, their title, or their years of experience. It shows up at the director level. It shows up at the VP level. I've seen it in GMs and in C-suite executives. The details are different, but the pattern is almost always the same: a professional who is operating at the wrong altitude for the role they're actually in.

> ***The thing that made you excellent at your last job is now the thing preventing you from being excellent at this one.***

Let me tell you about David Chen.

David was a VP of supply chain operations at a mid-size industrial company that had recently been acquired by a private equity group. The acquisition meant that everything was under a microscope: every hire required three levels of approval, every dollar spent was scrutinized, and David's team was right in the middle of a massive enterprise system implementation that kept getting delayed because the vendor had over-promised and the organization had underestimated the complexity by about a factor of three.

David had been in the role for about two years, but as he put it, it felt like five in another company. His team was spending 60 to 70% of their capacity on the implementation alone. When I asked him about the organization's biggest pain points, he could rattle them off instantly — unclear roles across departments, terrible cross-functional communication, and data quality issues that nobody wanted to own. "And we're smack in the middle of all three," he said. "We sit in the middle of it all."

He could see the forest. But he was spending his days on the floor, manually pulling inventory discrepancy reports that his operations managers should have been handling. He was reviewing individual journal entries. He was sitting in vendor calls that his directors should have been running. Not because he didn't trust his team. Because that's how he'd always operated — close to the ground, hands on, nothing slipping through.

David had a military background; he grew up as a military kid, moved around constantly, and had developed this remarkable ability to walk into chaos and create order. That's what had made him successful. But now that same instinct to be intimately involved in every detail was preventing him from operating at the level the PE firm needed from him. They didn't need someone checking inventory reports. They needed someone who could stand up in a board meeting and articulate a three-year operational strategy with confidence.

"My assumption is that you probably won't get the additional resources," I told him. "Because that feels like a long shot given everything you've said. I would really start to think about what your other options are here. Because just continuing as you're going is going to cause you to just get fed up."

And then I said, "You went about this like a senior manager or director would. We need to go about it like a VP would. You were doing it based off what worked before; it's just that those things aren't working at this altitude."

He took a breath. I could see it land.

"That's fair," he said. And then, "All right. What's the opportunity?"

Now we have something to work with.

David's version of the altitude problem was about going too deep — staying in the details because the details were where he'd built his career. But there's another version I see just as often, and it looks completely different.

Let me tell you about Nadia Karim.

Nadia was a senior director of product at a large technology company. She'd spent 10 years in the organization, steadily climbing from individual contributor to manager to senior manager to director. She knew the products inside and out. She knew the customers. She knew the stakeholders. She was, by every measure, a company institution.

And she was exhausted. Not from the work itself but from dragging 10 years of accumulated responsibilities behind her every single day.

When we sat down and mapped out where she was spending her time, the picture was striking. She was still attending the same product review meetings she'd attended as a senior manager. She was still personally reviewing design specs because she'd always been the one with the best eye for detail. She was still the person people pinged at 9 PM on Slack because she always responded. She had added every new responsibility from every promotion without ever subtracting anything from the level before.

I told her the ladder analogy, and she almost laughed. "That's exactly it," she said. "I'm carrying everything."

"What if advancement was all about giving up things that you really enjoy doing or are really good at for things that you might not enjoy or might not be good at. But you'll never know if you don't have the time to learn and practice."

She was quiet for a moment. "What if I start doing the new stuff and I don't like it?"

I hear this question often, and it's an important one. "In the beginning, you might not like it," I told her. "Because you're not good at it yet. And for people like you — people who've spent years being the expert

— not being good at something feels terrible. But that discomfort is the transition. It's not a warning sign. It's what growth actually feels like."

And then I said the thing that I think is the most important idea in this entire chapter: "Every promotion is an expert-to-beginner transition. Initially we talked about this as an operational problem — you're doing the wrong work. Now it's an identity crisis. You've been an expert for 10 years. And now your job is to be a beginner again. Not at everything but at the specific skills that this level requires. Strategic positioning. Organizational influence. Building leaders, not just managing contributors. Those are new muscles. And new muscles are sore before they're strong."

She pushed back. "But what if I let go of the design reviews and the quality drops?"

"Then that's coaching information," I said. "That tells you where to develop your team. But here's the thing — if they can't do it when you're standing right there, how can you be confident they can do it when you're not? That slightly uncomfortable process of watching someone struggle with something you could handle in 15 minutes — that's where their growth happens. And yours."

## THE REFRAME

This is not a personal failing. It's an environmental signal.

If you're feeling like you're working harder than ever and producing less, you're probably right. But it's not that your performance has dropped. It's because the job changed and you didn't change with it. Or more precisely, nobody told you how to change with it.

You spent years getting really good at something. You accumulated expertise, you built credibility, you developed instincts. And then someone promoted you, and now you need an entirely different set of skills. Strategic thinking instead of execution. Building people instead of building things. Influencing without authority instead of doing the work yourself.

The transition is disorienting. You've spent years accumulating expertise, and now the job is asking you to start building from scratch in areas where you have no muscle memory. "You're not starting over," I told Nadia. "You're building new skills on top of who you already are. You're not losing your expertise. You're building a new layer on top of it."

But here's the part that's hard to hear: your old expertise isn't just less valuable at the new altitude; in some cases, it's actively working against you. David's ability to dive into inventory data was a superpower at the director level. At the VP level, it was keeping him out of the rooms where decisions were being made about the future of his organization. Nadia's design review eye was legendary among her team. But every hour she spent reviewing specs was an hour she wasn't spending building relationships with the product VPs who would decide whether her org got funded next quarter.

I gave another leader the following advice and I want to pass it along here: "Learn enough about what your team is doing to be knowledgeable at your altitude, but don't be a clone of them. Let them shine as the experts. You shine as the person who builds and grows experts."

That reframes the whole identity question. Your job isn't to know everything. Your job is to know enough, at the right level, to make good decisions and develop the people who know the details. That's a completely different skill. And it's one you can build.

> ***Your old expertise isn't just less valuable at the new altitude. In some cases, it's actively working against you.***

I told one leader, "Think about your boss and your boss's boss. They do this to you all the time — they don't know all the details, so they send people to you. You're not expecting them to know everything. So why are you expecting yourself to know everything?" That's usually the moment the lights come on.

And here's the hardest part of the reframe. Sometimes the answer isn't about adjusting your altitude at all. Sometimes you're being asked to move a mountain with a teaspoon. Sometimes the organization has grossly underestimated what it takes, the resources aren't there, and the structure is broken. David's PE firm was expecting results from a team that was under-resourced by any honest accounting. Nadia's org had lost three senior people in eight months and hadn't backfilled any of them.

If you shift your altitude and try the new approach and the organization still won't meet you where you need them to — that's not failure, that's information. That's data you can use to make a real decision about whether this is the right environment for you.

## THE FRAMEWORK

This is where the work gets counterintuitive. Developing people means doing less, not more — and that's hard for leaders who got to this level by doing. These tools help you make the shift from solving to asking, from rescuing to releasing. Try them as experiments. The discomfort you feel is the point.

I'm going to give you four tools. I like things to be simple because, in my experience, we tend to be able to do simple things. And I like to treat things as experiments — try it and see if it works — because not every tool works for every person. We want to find the right set of things that work for you.

***Tool #1: The Altitude Dial.*** This is a tool that frankly can work for anyone at any level in any role. Imagine a dial with three settings. Below — work that someone on your team should be doing. You're doing it because it's comfortable, because you're faster at it, or because you don't trust them to get it right. At — work that actually requires your level. Your decision-making authority, your relationships, your strategic perspective. The stuff only you can do in your role. Above — work that stretches you toward the next level. The strategic thinking, the relationship building, the organizational positioning.

There's a version of the altitude problem that leaders don't talk about enough: the resource gap. Some leaders operate below their altitude not because they can't let go — but because they don't have enough people to hand the work to. They absorb the overload because they've learned, from experience or from culture, that asking for more headcount is a sign of weakness. It's not. Advocating for the resources your team needs is altitude-level work. The data that shows your team is at capacity, the business case for the additional hire, the ROI analysis — that's strategic

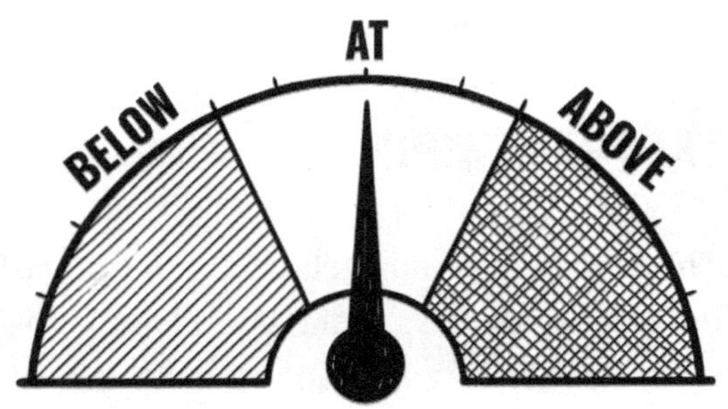


THE ALTITUDE DIAL

*If you can't see it, you can't argue with it.*

leadership, not complaining. The leader who silently drowns in work they shouldn't be doing isn't being strong. They're being the bottleneck.

Most professionals I work with, when they do this clearly, find that 40 to 60 percent of their time is spent on "below" work. That's not an exaggeration. I've seen VPs spending half their week on things their directors should be handling. And then they wonder why they don't have time for strategic thinking.

The goal isn't to eliminate all "below" work. Sometimes you need to dive in. The goal is to do it on purpose rather than by default. There's a big difference between intentionally going deep on something because it requires your involvement and reflexively doing it because that's what you've always done.

***Tool #2: The Capacity Thermometer.*** This one I developed from a conversation with David, and I've used it with dozens of people since. Think of one of those donation thermometers you see outside of churches during a fundraiser. Now, look at the year ahead and fill it up — fill it up with everything that's currently consuming your team's capacity. The implementation. The ongoing projects. The day-to-day operations. The fires. The meetings. All of it.

Now look at what's left.

Because here's what usually happens: people keep saying yes to new things without ever doing the math on what they've already committed to. The thermometer makes the invisible visible. It gives you something you can actually show to your boss and say, "Here's what we have. Here's what's left. If you want to add something, tell me what comes out."

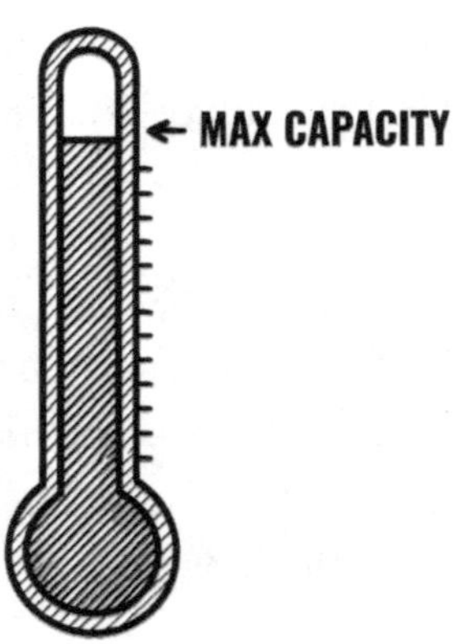


**THE CAPACITY THERMOMETER**

*Data, not a complaint.*

That's a fundamentally different conversation than "I can't do it, I'm overwhelmed." One is data. The other is a complaint. And data wins every time at the altitudes we're talking about. When David built his thermometer and showed it to his boss, his boss didn't push back. He couldn't. The picture was right there. You can argue with a feeling. You can't argue with a visual that shows 130 percent capacity utilization.

***Tool #3: The W-Questions Test.*** This comes from a delegation framework I've used for years. When you assign work, you get to set the who, what, where, when, and why. The how is up to the person doing the work. They get to figure out how to do it. If you're getting involved in the how, you're probably operating below your altitude.

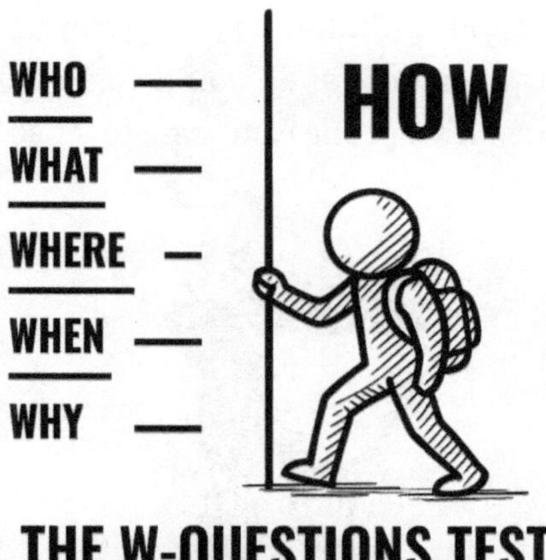


**THE W-QUESTIONS TEST**

*If you're in the How - you're at the wrong altitude.*

There's a critical caveat here. Even when someone asks you for help with the how, be careful. If you're too prescriptive, they're not actually learning how to do it themselves — you're just creating dependencies. So when they come to you and say, "How should I handle this?" try responding with, "What have you considered so far?" That one question shifts the interaction from you solving their problem to you coaching them through their own thinking. And coaching is your job at this altitude. Solving is not.

***Tool #4: Need to Know vs. Want to Know.*** For everything that crosses your desk, your inbox, your Slack, your meeting invites, ask one question: Do I need to know this, or do I want to know this? Need to know means it requires your decision, your authority, your involvement. Without you, it stops. Want to know means you're curious, you're interested, you'd like to be in the loop. But nothing actually stops if you're not.

If you're doing something because you like it but it's not the best use of your time, that's fine, but it has to go in the hobby category. Which means it can't be in the critical path. You can tinker around with it when you have the bandwidth. But if you're answering no to both "Is this something only I can do?" and "Do I gain anything other than it getting done?" — then it's a prime candidate to let go of.

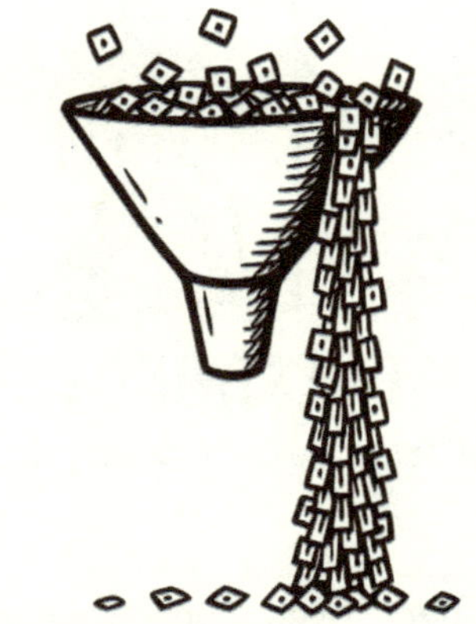

**NEED TO KNOW VS. WANT TO KNOW**

*Curious isn't critical.*

## THE EXPERIMENT

I like to treat things as experiments. Let's try it and see if it works. Not every tool works for every person. So here's what I want you to do — not eventually, not when the timing feels right, but this week.

The Altitude Log. For five business days, at the end of each day, take 10 minutes and write down the significant things you spent time on. Next to each one, mark it: Below, At, or Above your role level. Don't judge it. Don't try to fix it yet. Just observe.

At the end of the week, add it up. What percentage of your time was Below? What percentage was At? What percentage was Above? If the below number is higher than 30 percent, you have work to do. And you probably already knew that, but now you have data instead of a feeling.

Now ask yourself: What would have to change for me to shift just 10 percent from "below" to "at" or "above"?

That's it. Just 10 percent. Not a revolution. An experiment. Because here's what I've learned — from personal experience and from watching 100s of people try to change everything at once — going too big too fast means you just abandon it. It's like going from eating whatever you want to eating nothing but salads. By Wednesday you're ordering pizza.

Small shifts. Consistent practice. That's how altitude changes.

And then next week, try one more thing. Pick one task that's squarely in your "below" column — one that you enjoy, one that makes you feel capable and in control — and hand it to someone on your team. Give them the who, what, when, where, and why. Let them figure out the how. Don't check on it every four hours. Don't redo it after they're done. Let it go.

If they do it at 70% of the level you would have done it, that's a win. Because they'll get better. And you just got time back that you can invest in work that actually belongs at your altitude. That math compounds faster than you think.

## THE MIRROR

- What would you need to change right now for your team to function at 80% of its current level without you for two weeks? Not perfectly — just functionally. If you can't answer that question, that's the first thing to work on.

- What are you holding onto from your previous role that's giving you comfort but costing you growth? Be specific. Name the tasks. Name the meetings. Name the habits.

- When's the last time you said no to something that was below your altitude? What happened? If you can't remember, that tells you something.

- If your boss asked you right now what your strategic priorities are for the next quarter — not your team's projects, but your strategic priorities — could you answer in two sentences?

- What's the thing you keep doing that you know someone on your team could do, but you do it anyway because you're faster or because you do it better? What would it cost you to let them do it imperfectly for a while?

- Are you operating at this altitude because it's where you should be, or because it's where you're comfortable?

- What if, for every minute you spent on work below your altitude, you were taking a minute away from the career you actually want? Would you change how you spend your time tomorrow?

One more thing before we move on.

I worked with a leader who had just been recalibrated in his performance review — corporate speak for "you didn't meet the bar." He was frustrated. He was working incredibly hard. He felt like it was unfair.

I told him, "You may have been doing a great job at the level you were at. But now you're up here. Great is different. The bar is different. You need to recalibrate to your new altitude."

> ***The job didn't get harder. It changed. And different requires a different you — not a better version of the old one.***

And then I said something I'd say to you if you were sitting across from me right now: "You're not going to rewire your personality through this. That's not what we're doing, and that's not going to last. What we're doing is building new skills on top of who you already are. Every expert was a beginner at some point. You're just at the beginning of the next thing."

You don't have to become someone else. You just have to stop being the old version of yourself in a role that's asking for the next one.

That's the altitude problem. And once you see it, you can't unsee it.

Which is exactly the point.

## CHAPTER TWO

# THE IMPOSTER IN THE ROOM

*You're not faking it. You're using an outdated map.*

---

*"I keep waiting for someone to figure out that I don't actually know what I'm doing at this level."*

**— A VP, 18 months into a role she was headhunted for**

## THE PATTERN

Here's what surprises people about imposter syndrome: the higher you go, the worse it gets. You'd think that more evidence of competence would quiet the voice. It doesn't. It just gives the voice more creative material to work with. I've coached 100s of professionals, and I'd estimate that at least half of them — probably more — are carrying some version of this. The ones who seem the most confident are often the ones running the hardest to stay ahead of it.

It shows up in two ways. Some people over-prepare, over-deliver, and over-function — burning themselves out to make sure the mask never slips. Others go quiet — holding back contributions, shrinking in rooms where they belong, waiting for permission that's never coming. Same root. Different symptoms.

Let me tell you about Maya Patel.

Maya was 44 years old and recently promoted to SVP of product at a healthcare technology company. She'd spent two decades building her career across startups and enterprises. She'd led product launches that generated 100s of millions in revenue. She'd built teams from scratch and rebuilt teams that were broken. She had a track record that would make most people in her field envious.

And she was quietly convinced that it was only a matter of time before someone figured out that she didn't belong in the room.

Maya's 360 feedback told a very different story. The people around her — her peers, her direct reports, her cross-functional partners — rated her significantly higher than she rated herself across almost every category. Her peers called her one of the strongest strategic thinkers on the leadership team. Her direct reports said she was the best manager they'd ever worked for. One skip-level wrote that Maya was "the reason I stayed at this company."

And Maya sat across from me looking at these results like they were describing someone else.

"They must be being nice," she said. And she meant it.

Here's the thing about Maya's version of imposter syndrome: it didn't look like what you read about in articles. She wasn't paralyzed with self-doubt. She wasn't hiding in the corner. She was compensating. Her anxiety drove her to over-prepare for everything — creating presentations that were three times longer than they needed to be, researching every possible question that might come up in a meeting, arriving 45 minutes early to rehearse her talking points. The work product was often thrown away because it wasn't needed at that level of detail. But not doing it felt dangerous.

She couldn't stop at "good enough" because good enough felt like the moment the mask would slip.

Here's the thing about high-performing imposters: they don't look like imposters from the outside. They look like the hardest-working person in the room, which they often are. And that's the trap. Because the over-preparation, the over-delivery, and the obsessive attention to detail — those all look like excellence from the outside. Nobody is going to tap you on the shoulder and say, "Hey, you know you don't need to do all of that, right?"

The machine keeps running because the machine keeps producing. But inside the machine, something is slowly burning out.

When I showed Maya the gap between her self-ratings and everyone else's, she did what I've seen dozens of high performers do: she rationalized it. "They're probably being generous because they know the feedback goes to me." Then, "Maybe they just haven't seen me in the situations where I struggle." Then, "I think they're rating the work product, not me."

Three defenses in 30 seconds. Each one designed to protect the same belief: that the imposter narrative was the accurate one and the data was somehow wrong. This is what makes imposter syndrome so persistent. It's not that people lack evidence to the contrary. It's that they've built an immune system that rejects any evidence that contradicts the story.

I told her, "You just did something really interesting. I gave you data from 12 people who know your work intimately, and you spent 30 seconds explaining why all 12 of them are wrong and you're right. Does that sound like the kind of analysis you'd accept in any other domain?"

She laughed. It was the kind of laugh that meant something just landed.

"If a product manager came to me with survey data from 12 customers and then told me the data was wrong because the customers were probably being nice," she said, "I'd send them back to do more work."

"Exactly," I said. "So why is the standard different when the data is about you?"

> ***Imposter syndrome doesn't always look like self-doubt. Sometimes it looks like the hardest-working person in the room. Sometimes it looks like the quietest.***

I want to share a second version of this because it's equally common and looks completely different.

Let me tell you about Chris Webber.

Chris was a senior director of analytics at a professional services firm, in his mid-forties with 20-plus years of experience. He'd been moved around the organization several times — different teams, different leaders, different mandates. He was sharp, thorough, and deeply competent. And he brought a very specific concern to coaching: he didn't feel like people listened to him in leadership meetings.

When we dug into it, what emerged wasn't a communication problem. It was a pattern that he didn't even realize he was repeating.

In meetings, Chris absorbed everything. He listened intently. He processed information. He took notes. He formulated thoughts. But by the time he'd cleared his own internal bar for whether his contribution was good enough to say out loud, the moment had passed. The conversation had moved on. And his silence — which felt to him like thoughtfulness — registered to everyone else as either disengagement or, worse, having nothing to add.

I asked him something that made him uncomfortable: "Have you noticed this when you're in other conversations and someone is not saying anything? What do you think about them?"

He paused. "I guess... I don't really think about them."

"Exactly," I said."That's the best case. The best case when you're silent is that you're invisible. People leave the meeting and think, 'Was Chris there? Did he say something? I don't remember.' You don't make a mark. And invisible people don't get promoted. They don't get invited to the next meeting. They don't get considered for the high-visibility project."

The imposter wasn't making him quiet because he had nothing to say. It was making him quiet because he was afraid that what he said wouldn't be good enough. So he kept processing. And the more he processed without contributing, the more he confirmed his own fear that he didn't have anything worth adding. It was a perfect, self-reinforcing loop. And he had no idea he was repeating it.

Then I asked him something else: "When was the last time you updated your leadership team about a win? Not your team's work, but your specific contribution?"

He couldn't remember.

"So you're invisible in meetings, and you're not surfacing your contributions outside of meetings. And then you're frustrated that people don't recognize your value." I let that sit for a moment. "Do you see how you're creating the exact situation you're complaining about?"

That one landed hard. But it needed to.

Chris had been telling himself that his value would eventually be recognized through the quality of his work. That's a story that sounds noble: "Let the work speak for itself." But at his altitude, the work doesn't speak. You have to speak for it. And the imposter was the thing keeping his mouth shut.

We spent several sessions building what I call his "in-the-moment muscles" — the ability to formulate a thought and say it without running it through every possible filter first. I told him to prepare one specific contribution for each important meeting. Not an elaborate analysis. Just one observation or perspective that he could drop in early, before his processing instinct had time to paralyze him.

The first time he tried it, he told me it felt like jumping off a diving board. "I just said it before I could stop myself." And nobody laughed. Nobody dismissed him. In fact, two people built on his point and the conversation went in a productive direction because of it.

"That's the data point," I told him. "The bar for contributing is so much lower than the bar you've set for yourself. You've been waiting to have the perfect thing to say. Everyone else is just saying things."

## THE REFRAME

Here's what I've come to understand about imposter syndrome after sitting with 100s of professionals who experience it: it's almost always an identity lag.

What I mean is this. Your professional identity — the internal picture of who you are, what you're capable of, and where you belong — takes 6 to 18 months to catch up after a significant change. You got the new title, the new scope, and the new expectations. But the person inside is still measuring themselves against the standards of who they used to be.

## THE OUTDATED MAP

*The map got you here. It won't get you there.*

Maya was measuring herself against the standard of a director-level product leader who needed to be the most prepared person in every meeting. At the SVP level, that wasn't just unnecessary — it was counterproductive. Her over-preparation was actually slowing down decisions because she was always the one asking for more time, more data, more analysis before committing.

Chris was measuring himself against a culture where he had decades of credibility banked. In his current role, reporting to new leadership after a reorg, he was starting that credibility account from a much lower balance. And the gap between his internal sense of his value and the recognition that he was receiving felt like fraud. It wasn't fraud. It was a recalibration period. But it felt identical.

> ***Imposter syndrome is not evidence that you don't belong. It's evidence that your identity hasn't caught up to your reality.***

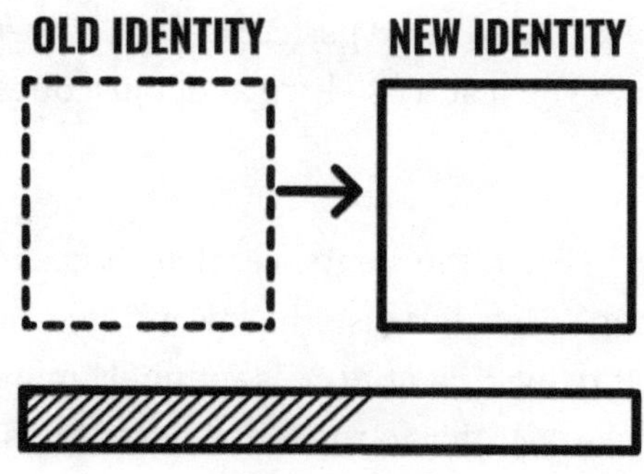


**6-18 MONTHS**

**THE IDENTITY UPDATE**

*Your title changed. Your internal map takes 6-18 months to follow.*

The other reframe I want to offer is about perfectionism. Because in my experience, imposter syndrome and perfectionism are two masks on the same face.

The imposter says, "I'm not good enough." Perfectionism says, "So I have to be perfect to compensate." They feed each other in a loop that looks like high performance from the outside but feels like a treadmill on the inside.

I sat with Ben in his final coaching session. He had spent months working on finding his non-negotiables, the things he wasn't willing to compromise on in family, work, and self. He'd made real progress across every dimension. And then he said something that stopped me.

"Not there yet. My goal is to at least find what good looks like. They're not going to be perfect."

Then he said: "I don't need to be perfect in a lot of these things. Even at home, sometimes you just try so hard and it just doesn't work. Good is enough."

Good is enough. That's the sentence that breaks the imposter-perfectionism loop. Not because it lowers the bar. Because it acknowledges that delivering at 80% is infinitely more valuable than endlessly polishing something to 100% that never ships. And that extra hour you spent getting from 80 to 95? Nobody noticed. But you know what they did notice? That you were late to your daughter's school event. That you missed the deadline on the strategic initiative because you were perfecting the operational report. That you were exhausted and sharp in a meeting where your composure actually mattered.

Perfectionism doesn't protect you. It redirects your effort from where it's needed to where it's comfortable. And "comfortable" for a perfectionist means the zone where they already know they're excellent, which, as we talked about in Chapter 1, is usually the wrong altitude.

I want to address one more flavor of this because I see it constantly and people rarely name it.

Some professionals don't have imposter syndrome in the classic sense. They don't doubt their competence. What they doubt is their fit. They walk into a leadership meeting and look around the room and think, "I don't operate like these people." They're quieter, more direct, or less polished. Or they came from a different background, a different culture, or a different kind of company. And the mismatch between how they operate and how the people around them operate gets interpreted as evidence that they don't belong.

It's not evidence that you don't belong. It's evidence that you're different. And different is often exactly what the organization needs, even if the organization doesn't know it yet.

I told Chris, "Your preparation muscles are already strong. We don't need to build those. What we need to start building are your in-the-moment muscles — the ability to formulate a thought and say it without running it through 17 filters first. That's going to be uncomfortable. It's supposed to be. That discomfort is the muscle growing."

He pushed back: "But what if I say something that's wrong? Or not fully thought through?"

I said, "Look around the room next time you're in one of those meetings. How many things do other people say that are partially formed or not quite right or thinking out loud? Most of what gets said in meetings is not polished. It's directional. You're holding yourself to a standard that nobody else in the room is meeting — and they're getting promoted while you're staying invisible."

That one stung. But it was the truth he needed to hear. His imposter wasn't protecting him from embarrassment; it was guaranteeing his irrelevance. And that's the cruelest trick imposter syndrome plays: it convinces you that silence is safety when silence is actually the thing that's most dangerous to your career.

> ***The imposter doesn't protect you from failure. It protects you from being seen. And being seen is the only way forward.***

# THE IMPOSTER MACHINE

*The immune system that rejects evidence.*

## THE FRAMEWORK

Imposter syndrome doesn't respond to pep talks. It responds to evidence. These three tools are designed to generate that evidence — to close the gap between the outdated map you're navigating with and the territory you're actually in. They're not about building confidence. They're about updating your operating system so confidence becomes unnecessary.

***Tool #1: The Identity Update.*** Write down the role you had two years ago. Next to it, write down the skills, behaviors, and standards that made you successful in that role. Now do the same for your current role. Compare the two lists. Where are you still operating from the old one?

Those gaps aren't weaknesses — they're update opportunities. You don't need a personality transplant. You need a software update. Maya's old operating system said, "be the most prepared person in the room." Her new one needed to say, "be the person who asks the right question at the right moment." Chris's old system said, "process everything thoroughly before speaking." His new one needed to say, "offer a perspective early and let the room build on it."

***Tool #2: The 80% Rule.*** For one week, before you start any significant task, ask yourself, "What would 80% look like on this?" Then deliver that. See what happens. Track the outcomes. Did anyone notice the difference between your 80% and your usual 100? My prediction: they won't. And the time you save can go toward the strategic work that actually moves the team, the organization, and your career forward.

This isn't about lowering your standards. It's about being strategic about where you deploy your perfectionism. Some things deserve 100%. Most don't.

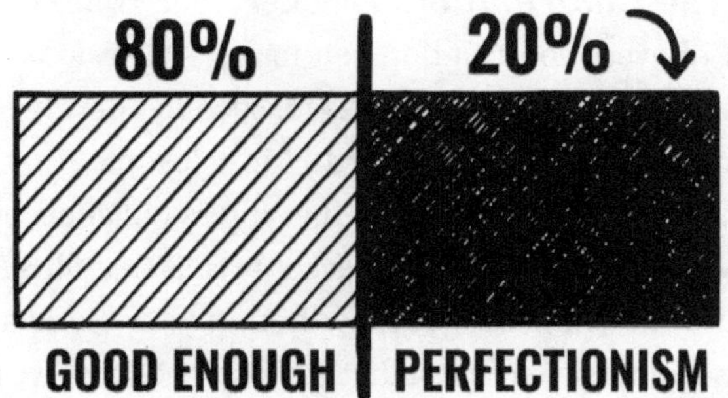


**THE 80% RULE**

*Good enough is a strategy, not a compromise.*

***Tool #3: The Permission Audit.*** Write down three things you're waiting for permission to do. Then ask yourself: Who exactly am I waiting for? What would happen if I just did it?

In my experience, most professionals are waiting for permission that nobody is going to give them. Not because people don't want them to do the thing. But because nobody else is thinking about it. I asked a leader once, "Are you looking for me to give you permission to get rid of your uncertainty?" He laughed because that's exactly what he was doing. He didn't need permission. He needed someone to point out that the only person withholding it was himself.

You have more agency in your situation than you think you do. Much more. The imposter convinces you that you need authorization from some external source before you can act. You don't. Act first. Adjust second. That's how people at your altitude operate.

***Tool #4: The Contribution Tracker.*** For two weeks, keep a running list of every contribution you make — decisions influenced, problems solved, perspectives offered, people developed. Not a gratitude journal. A factual record. Most people with imposter syndrome have a selective memory that filters out their own impact and amplifies everyone else's. The tracker breaks that filter. When you see 40 contributions in two weeks written in your own handwriting, it's harder to maintain the fiction that you don't belong. I've had clients look at their list after two weeks and say, "I had no idea I was doing this much." They weren't doing more. They were finally seeing what was already there.

## THE EXPERIMENT

There are two experiments this week. Both are small but will feel bigger than they are.

Experiment one: In one meeting, speak up within the first five minutes with an observation or a perspective. Not a question. Not a request for clarification. A point of view. It doesn't have to be brilliant. It just has to be yours. Say it before your internal filter has time to kill it. Notice how people respond. My prediction: they'll engage with it. And you'll realize that the bar for contributing is much lower than the bar you've set for yourself.

Experiment two: For one task this week, deliberately deliver at 80%. Don't add the extra analysis. Don't stay late polishing the deck. Don't run the numbers one more time. Ship it at 80% and observe what happens. Track what you do with the time you saved. That's the real data point — not whether anyone noticed the quality difference, but what became possible when you stopped over-investing in diminishing returns.

## THE MIRROR

- What would you do differently if you knew, with certainty, that you belonged in the room? Write down three specific things. Those are your action items.
- Where is your perfectionism protecting you from the discomfort of being a beginner? Name the specific tasks where you over-invest because being less than excellent feels threatening.

- What's the worst thing that would actually happen if you delivered at 80%? Has that worst case ever actually materialized? In your entire career?

- Who do you compare yourself to? Are they actually at the same career stage, or are you measuring yourself against someone with 15 more years of context and pretending the comparison is fair?

- If you trusted that you were enough for this role — not perfect, just enough — what would you stop doing? That's your over-functioning list, and it's probably longer than you think.

- When's the last time you asked for feedback and the feedback was better than you expected? What did you do with that information? If the answer is "dismissed it," ask yourself why.

- How much of your energy goes toward proving you belong versus actually doing the work? Be honest about the ratio. It's probably not where you want it to be.

## CHAPTER THREE

# THE STORIES YOU'RE TELLING YOURSELF

*How to separate facts from assumptions and emotions — and why it matters*

---

*"I know she's trying to undermine me. Everything she does confirms it."*

**— A senior leader, two conversations before discovering she was completely wrong**

## THE PATTERN

If there's one thing I do more than anything else in coaching, it's this: I help people separate what actually happened from the story they built around it. It sounds simple and it's the hardest thing in the book.

We all do it. Something happens — a comment in a meeting, an email that felt short, a decision that went the other way — and within minutes, we've constructed an entire narrative about what it means. The narrative feels like truth. It's not. It's a rough draft written by our emotions and edited by our ego. And most professionals I work with are making real decisions based on rough drafts they've never bothered to fact-check.

**THE ROUGH DRAFT**

*Same facts. Different story.*

Let me tell you about Claire Whitfield.

Claire came to a session furious. She was a senior director of brand strategy at a consumer packaged goods company. She was sharp, meticulous, and deeply committed to her work. She'd been in the role for three years and had built her team into one of the highest-performing groups in the organization. She took pride in that. And she was convinced that a peer — a woman named Andrea on the commercial team — was territorial, competitive, and systematically trying to be the only one with direct access to their shared VP.

Claire had evidence. Andrea had taken on responsibilities that used to be shared, communicated directly with the VP without copying Claire, and had been in meetings that Claire wasn't invited to. Claire had been tracking this for weeks and had built an airtight case in her mind.

I listened. And then I asked her, "How much of what you just told me is fact, and how much is a story you've built around the facts?"

She paused.

That pause is everything. It's the moment where the certainty cracks just enough to let a different possibility in.

Here's what was factual: Andrea had taken on certain responsibilities. Andrea communicated directly with the VP. Andrea had been in meetings Claire wasn't in. All observable. All true. But everything else — the intent, the motivation, the territorial power play — was Claire's construction. She had organized real events into a narrative that confirmed her suspicion. It was a compelling story. It felt true. But a feeling isn't a fact, no matter how strongly we feel it.

> ***If we're having an emotional reaction to someone, it's usually because we're expecting them to be something that they are not.***

I told Claire something I tell leaders at these altitudes all the time: "There are three things people always underestimate. Self-interest, ego, and competition."

Let me unpack this because it's a framework that I come back to so often that my regular clients start rolling their eyes when they hear it. But it keeps being true, so I keep saying it.

**THE THREE FORCES**

*Always present. Rarely named.*

Self-interest means that everyone is, to some degree, optimizing for their own outcome. That doesn't make them bad. It makes them human. If they stopped paying you tomorrow, you wouldn't come in the next day. That's self-interest. It's the exchange of value that drives every professional relationship, and pretending it doesn't exist is naïveté, not kindness.

Ego means that people care how they're perceived, sometimes more than they care about the actual outcome. They'll fight for territory not because the territory matters but because losing it feels like a public diminishment. They'll resist a good idea because it wasn't their idea.

Competition means that, at senior levels, people are jockeying — for resources, for attention, for the next promotion, for proximity to power. Sometimes it's healthy. Sometimes it's territorial. But it's always present.

I said to Claire, "Your assumption about Andrea wanting to be the only one with VP access? That's competition. But you're assuming her competitive muscle is really strong when it might be something very different. It could be that, throughout her career, she's had to push through to get what she wants. Maybe people constantly tried to take territory from her. So she's protective and defensive. Not because she's against you, but because she's used to having to fight for everything."

Claire's whole posture changed. "I hadn't thought about it that way."

"Of course you hadn't," I said. "Because when we're in an emotional reaction, we're not doing analysis. We're doing prosecution. We're building a case, not seeking understanding."

I want to share a different version of this because it illustrates something critical about the stories that we miss.

Let me tell you about Tamara Osei.

Tamara was a senior director of engineering at a large technology company. She'd spent most of her career in direct, transparent cultures — the kind of place where you say what you mean, you disagree openly in meetings, and nobody takes it personally. She was good at that game. She thrived in it.

Then she moved to a company where the game was completely different.

People smiled and said everything was fine. They agreed in the meeting and disagreed in the hallway. Feedback didn't come to your face; it went to your manager behind your back. And Tamara, with her direct-culture operating system, was missing every signal.

Her manager would ask things like, "So, how are things with your team? How's your relationship with Raj?" And Tamara would say, "I think it's going well." She answered the question at face value. It didn't occur to her that the question itself was the signal.

I told her, "Anytime someone asks you something like that about someone specifically, they're almost always fishing. Why would they ask you about one person by name unless there's something behind it?"

She stared at me. "Really?"

"I see it all the time now," I said. "But it took a long time for me to notice it. And then once you start watching for it, you see it more often than you'd think."

She said something that stuck with me: "My brain had to adapt to this. It was too direct from point A to point B. It was incapable of seeing what was actually happening."

This isn't a flaw in Tamara. It's a mismatch between her operating assumptions and the culture she was actually in. She was telling herself a story: "People communicate directly." That story was true in her previous company. It was completely false in her current one. And because the story was wrong, she was missing critical information for months — feedback going to her manager that she never heard, concerns being raised in rooms she wasn't in, and a reputation forming that she had no visibility into.

The story you tell yourself about how the world works is the lens through which you see everything. And if that lens is calibrated for the wrong environment, you're going to misread every signal that comes your way.

Tamara eventually adapted. It took months of deliberate practice — learning to read between the lines, learning to notice when a question wasn't really a question, learning to follow up on conversations that felt innocuous but weren't. She told me, "I feel like I learned a second language." And in a real way, she had. Organizational communication is a language, and every company has its own dialect.

The thing that helped her most was something counterintuitive: instead of getting frustrated that people weren't being direct with her, she got curious about why they communicated the way they did. What was the culture protecting? What had happened in the organization's history that made indirect communication feel safer? When she approached it as anthropology instead of annoyance, she started seeing patterns she'd been completely blind to.

And here's the piece that connects Tamara's story to Claire's: they were both telling themselves stories. Claire was telling herself a story about Andrea's intent. Tamara was telling herself a story about how communication works. Both stories were wrong. Both stories were costing them something significant. And both stories felt absolutely, unquestionably true.

That's the dangerous thing about our narratives. The false ones feel exactly as true as the real ones. There's no internal alarm that goes off and says, "Hey, this one's an assumption, not a fact." They all feel like facts. Which is why you need a process to separate them.

## THE REFRAME

The reframe is the single most used coaching tool across everything I do. And the core of it is stunningly simple: separate what you know from what you're making up.

We all construct stories constantly. It's how our brains work. We take incomplete information and fill in the gaps with assumptions that feel like truth. The problem isn't that we do it — we can't stop doing it, it's literally how human cognition functions. The problem is that we treat the story as if it's fact and then make decisions based on it.

Claire was about to launch a campaign to outmaneuver Andrea based entirely on a narrative. Think about the energy that would have consumed. Think about the damage to a relationship that might actually have been salvageable. Think about how the VP would have perceived Claire if she'd started playing political chess based on an assumption she never bothered to verify.

The single most powerful reframe question I've found is this: "What changed?"

Instead of arguing about whether someone's behavior is hostile or benign, ask what's different between when things were working and when they stopped. "What changed?" is disarming because it's not an accusation. It's curiosity. And curiosity almost always produces better information than confrontation. People can defend against accusations. They cannot defend against genuine curiosity.

**THE PROSECUTOR**

*You've been building a case. Time to check the evidence.*

I use this constantly. When someone comes in frustrated about a direct report's performance: "What changed? Were they always like this, or did something shift?" When someone is upset about a peer relationship: "What changed between when you two were working well together and now?" When someone is anxious about their own performance: "What changed between when you felt confident and now?"

The answer is almost always more interesting than the complaint.

A director came to me once frustrated that his boss had given a key project to a peer instead of him. He was building a case: the peer was less qualified and the decision was political, which was proof that his boss didn't value his contributions. The story was airtight. And getting tighter every day as he collected more evidence to support it.

I asked him, "What changed between when your boss gave you the last big project and now?"

He started to answer with his story, and I stopped him. "Not what you think is going on. What actually changed? In the team, in the priorities, in your boss's world?"

He thought about it. Really thought. And what came out was: his boss had just come under significant pressure from the board about a related initiative. The peer who got the project had a specific client relationship that was relevant. And his boss had mentioned, offhand, three months ago, that he wanted to "spread the exposure around" for development purposes.

None of that fit the story he'd been telling. All of it fit the actual situation. The decision wasn't a judgment on his value. It was a combination of board pressure, a relevant relationship, and a development philosophy that his boss had literally told him about. He just hadn't heard it because he wasn't listening for it.

"So the story you've been carrying around for two weeks — the one that's been eating your energy and poisoning your relationship with your peer — was based on an assumption you could have checked with a single conversation," I said.

He nodded. "That's embarrassing."

"It's not embarrassing," I said. "It's human. We all do it. The question is how long you let the story run before you check it."

> ***People can defend against accusations. They cannot defend against genuine curiosity.***

There's one more piece to this reframe that I want to address directly because it's the one professionals struggle with the most.

The place people miss this most is with their own leaders. They think, "Oh, they're looking out for me." And I have to be honest with them: I can tell you they're not. Not entirely. It doesn't mean they don't care about you. But that is not their primary concern. I can promise you that.

This isn't cynicism. It's calibration. There's a profound difference between assuming good intent and being naïve about human motivation. You can assume that people generally mean well while also accounting for the fact that everyone — including you and me — is operating with some degree of self-interest. When you calibrate for that, you stop being surprised by behavior that used to confuse you. You stop taking things personally that were never about you. And you start making better decisions because you're working with more accurate data about the people around you.

## THE FRAMEWORK

Most of the leaders I work with aren't making bad decisions because they lack intelligence. They're making them because they've built an airtight case on top of assumptions they've never tested. These tools help you take the case apart — separate what's real from what you've constructed — and make decisions based on what's actually there.

I'm going to give you three tools here. They're not about eliminating assumptions — you can't. They're about separating what you know from what you're making up, so you stop making decisions based on stories you've never verified. These tools close that gap.

***Tool #1: The Facts / Assumptions / Emotions Audit.*** This is the single most useful diagnostic I know. Take any situation that feels charged. Draw three columns. In the first column, write only the observable facts — things a camera would record. No interpretation. No inference. Just what happened. In the second column, write your assumptions — what you're interpreting, inferring, or guessing about intent, motivation, or meaning. In the third, write what you're feeling.

> ***The story you're telling yourself about someone else's intent is almost certainly incomplete. And you're making decisions based on the incomplete version.***

Claire's facts were three items long. Her assumptions were a page. She was making career-defining decisions based on the page.

**FACTS / ASSUMPTIONS / EMOTIONS**

*The story was mostly assumptions.*

Do this exercise before any conversation where you feel emotional. It takes five minutes. It will save you from saying things you'll regret and from responding to situations that don't actually exist.

***Tool #2: The Ego-Interest-Competition Lens.*** Before reacting to anyone's behavior at your altitude, filter it through three questions: Is self-interest a factor here? Is ego involved? Is competition at play? These aren't judgments. They're calibration tools. If you assume someone is acting purely out of goodwill and they're actually acting out of self-interest, you'll misread every signal they send. If you assume competition isn't a factor and it is, you'll be blindsided when someone claims territory you thought was yours.

I use this with nearly every client at the director level and above. Because failing to account for these forces leads to naïveté. And naïveté at senior levels can be dangerous.

***Tool #3: The "What Changed?" Redirect.*** The next time you're in a conversation that's becoming adversarial — whether it's a performance discussion, a peer conflict, or a strategy disagreement — replace your instinct to argue your position with a single question: "What changed?" It shifts the conversation from debate to discovery. It signals curiosity instead of confrontation. And it usually produces an answer that neither of you expected.

***Tool #4: The Fishing Detector.*** This isn't a daily practice — but when you need it, it's decisive. When someone above you asks about a specific person or a specific situation unprompted, assume they're fishing until proven otherwise. The appropriate response is not to answer the surface question. It's to answer carefully, then go find out what prompted the question. Because something prompted it. It always does.

## THE EXPERIMENT

The next time you have a strong emotional reaction to a colleague's behavior – frustration, anger, suspicion, hurt – before you respond, sit down and do the three-column exercise: Facts, Assumptions, and Emotions. Take five minutes, and write it out.

Then ask yourself: If my worst assumptions were wrong, what would I do differently?

Try that approach instead. Just once. See what happens. My prediction: the conversation will go better than it would have, and you'll learn something about the situation that your emotional reaction was preventing you from seeing.

And here's a second experiment: this week, when you find yourself frustrated or confused by someone's behavior, try the "What changed?" question. Not accusatorily. With real curiosity. "I noticed things feel different between us lately. What changed?" Then watch what it opens up.

## THE MIRROR

- What story have you been telling yourself about someone at work that you've never actually verified? What would it take to verify it?

- When's the last time your assumption about someone's intent turned out to be completely wrong? What did that experience teach you? Did you apply that lesson, or did you go right back to assumption-making?

- Are you giving someone the benefit of the doubt, or are you building a case? Be honest. Building a case feels like being thorough. It's not. It's prosecution.

- What would "curious" look like in the situation that's frustrating you most right now? What would you ask if you truly didn't know the answer?

- Where are you underestimating the role of self-interest, ego, or competition in a relationship that's confusing you?

- What signals might you be missing because your operating assumptions are calibrated for a different culture, a different company, or a different era of your career?

- If someone were telling the story about you — building assumptions about your behavior and your intent without asking — what would they get wrong? And what does that tell you about the stories you're building about others?

## CHAPTER FOUR

# THE DENTIST TRAP

*When being too good at your job holds you back*

---

*"People come to me for everything. I should feel good about that, but it's starting to feel like a cage."*

**— A director, three years in the same role**

## THE PATTERN

You'll find that I use this analogy often, so let me lay it out properly.

How often do you think about your dentist? Not often, right? You think about them when you have a problem — a toothache, a cleaning, a crown that needs replacing. And when that problem is solved, you put them back on the shelf and don't think about them again until the next problem. There's nothing wrong with your dentist. You might love your dentist. But they're only top of mind when their specific expertise is needed.

This is what happens to professionals who are extremely good at one thing. Their credibility gets anchored in that ability. And when other conversations come up — strategic conversations, leadership conversations, cross-functional opportunities — they are left out. People aren't excluding them on purpose. They just don't think of them because their reputation is cemented in the expertise, not in the broader leadership.

You become the dentist. And the dentist never gets invited to the strategy meeting.

> ***They're not excluding you. They just don't think of you because you've never given them a reason to think of you beyond your expertise.***

# THE DENTIST

***Your tools became your cage.***

Let me tell you about Marcus Rivera.

Marcus was a director of client operations at a mid-size software company. He was the person who could fix anything. When a customer escalation was on fire, Marcus got the call. When a project was off the rails, Marcus got pulled in. When a new team member needed mentoring, they were pointed to Marcus. When cross-functional processes broke down, Marcus was the one who sat in the room and put them back together.

He was the firefighter, the fixer, the person everyone depended on. And he couldn't figure out why he kept getting passed over for a VP role.

The answer was hiding in plain sight. Marcus had made himself so essential to the day-to-day operations that nobody could imagine the team functioning without him in that role. Promoting him would leave a hole that nobody knew how to fill — because Marcus had never developed anyone to fill it. He'd never built the bench. He was too busy catching every ball himself to teach anyone else how to play.

When I laid this out for him, he resisted at first. "But the clients don't care about my team's development. They care about results. I can't let my team stumble with a major account."

Fair point. I asked him the question that usually changes the conversation: "If you weren't available — if you were on a flight, in the hospital, unreachable for 48 hours — what would happen?"

Long pause.

"It would be rough," he said.

"That's the problem," I said. "Not that it would be rough. But that you've been in this role for three years and it would still be rough. What does that tell you about what you've been building?"

He sat with that. It wasn't comfortable.

"But I'm delivering results," he said. "My team hits every number."

"Your team hits every number because you're personally catching every ball that drops," I said. "That's not your team hitting numbers. That's you hitting numbers with an audience."

**THE FIXER**

*The heroism that creates the dependency.*

I could see him processing that. It's a hard distinction to accept when you're the leader who's proud of their results. But there's a meaningful difference between a team that performs because they're developed and a team that performs because their leader is personally doing the critical work. The first team survives a leadership change. The second one doesn't. And the people who decide promotions know the difference, even if they can't always articulate it.

I told Marcus, "The leaders above you are looking at two things. Are the results there? Yes. Could this organization function without Marcus? They're not sure. And that uncertainty is what's keeping you where you are."

Here's where it gets deeper — the part most leadership books skip.

When I pushed Marcus further, I told him something he didn't want to hear: "You like to be needed."

He thought about it for a minute. And then he nodded. "Yeah. I do."

That's the uncomfortable truth about why some leaders can't delegate. It's not about trust — they'll tell you that they trust their team. It's not about quality — they'll acknowledge that other people can do good work. It's about identity. Being the fixer, the rescuer, the person everyone comes to — that's how Marcus knew he mattered. Every time someone came to him with a problem and he solved it, he got a little hit of validation. And over the years, that had become the cornerstone of his professional self-worth.

This shows up in a specific behavioral pattern that I see so often it's almost a diagnostic: the Friday rescue mission. I worked with a leader in a different organization — we'll call her Denise — who was spending every Friday afternoon sitting down with her underperformers, going through their work, getting it back on track before the end of the week. Hours. Every single Friday.

I told her, "What's happening here is you're training them that less and less effort is okay because you'll always be there to bail them out. You're creating this codependency where they do the minimum, and then Denise sits down with them and spends hours getting it on the rails. And then next week, it happens again. And the week after that."

The word "codependency" hit her differently than "delegation problem." Because delegation sounds like a skill gap. Codependency sounds like what it actually is: a relationship pattern that's serving a need in both parties, and neither party wants to change.

For Denise, the rescue gave her purpose. It made her feel essential. For her underperformers, it removed accountability. Why push yourself when your boss will fix it anyway?

It was a system. And like all systems, it would keep running until someone deliberately broke it.

This shows up differently for high performers who aren't leaders.

Let me tell you about Raj Mehta.

Raj was a senior individual contributor at a technology company. He was brilliant at what he did — specifically, AI and machine learning applications. And he had become so identified with that domain that the organization literally couldn't think of him without thinking of AI.

His name and the topic were fused. Which was great, until he told his manager he wanted to be involved in broader strategic initiatives beyond just the AI work. His manager's response was essentially: "Sure, when there's an opportunity." Which, as anyone who's been in a corporate environment knows, means "probably never."

Raj was pigeonholed. Not because anyone disrespected him or wanted to limit him. Because he was so valuable in his niche that the organization couldn't afford to let him out of it. He was their dentist. And the dentist doesn't get to perform heart surgery, no matter how interested he is in cardiology.

The fix for Raj wasn't waiting for his manager to create the opportunity. It was creating the opportunity himself — offering perspectives in meetings that went beyond AI, building relationships with leaders in other functions, and volunteering for a cross-functional initiative where his expertise was relevant but not the centerpiece. Slowly, deliberately, expanding how people thought of him.

That's the escape route from the dentist trap. You can't wait for people to see you differently. You have to give them a reason to.

## THE REFRAME

There's another metaphor I use with leaders who can't step back: the pitcher and the coach.

You can't develop your team while you're on the mound throwing every pitch. At some point, you have to step off the field and into the dugout. Your job is to prepare people, set them up, watch them play, and coach them between innings. Even if they don't throw as well as you. Even if they give up a few runs. Because if they never throw, they never get better. And if they never get better, you never move.

## THE PITCHER AND THE COACH

***Step off the mound.***

The question you have to answer clearly: If you got promoted tomorrow, could your team survive for 60 days? If the answer is no, then that's not a reflection of your team's limitations. That's a reflection of your leadership. And it's probably the single biggest thing holding you back from the next level.

Because here's what leaders above you are thinking — whether they say it or not: "If I promote Marcus, who runs client operations? Nobody can do what he does." And they mean that as a compliment. But the effect is a cage. You've made yourself irreplaceable. And irreplaceable people don't get promoted. They get depended on.

I told another leader something that reframed the whole thing for him. He was talking about how he was irreplaceable at work. And I said, "Actually, we want it to be the other way around. You want to be replaceable at work. That means you've built something that works without you. That's a sign of great leadership, not a sign of diminished value."

> ***Irreplaceable people don't get promoted.***
> ***They get depended on.***

There's one more thing about the dentist trap, because it's the piece that makes people most uncomfortable. The trap isn't just about career stagnation. It's about what happens to your team when you're the one catching every ball.

I worked with a leader who had been a field operations expert for over a decade. He was the person who could walk into any site and diagnose problems faster than anyone. The day after we talked about the fixer pattern, he went right back to fixing. There was a situation, so he dove in. It was fast. It wasn't a big time loss, but he did it.

When he told me, he was almost sheepish about it. "I know. I know."

"The issue isn't this one instance," I said. "The issue is the signal. Every time you dive in, your team gets two messages. First: I don't fully trust you to handle this. Second: If it's really important, I'll do it myself. And those messages accumulate. Over months and years, they create a team that has learned helplessness. Not because they're incapable, but because their leader's behavior has trained them that the boss will always come to the rescue."

He said, "I have people who've already taken the torch out of my hands without me giving it to them." Which told me something important: the talent was there. The capability was there. The issue wasn't his team. The issue was his ego — and I mean that with compassion. His identity as the fixer was competing with his team's need to grow. And every time his identity won, his team lost a development opportunity.

## THE FRAMEWORK

The Dentist Trap is a cage you build yourself — one helpful act at a time. These tools help you see the cage, test which bars are real, and start creating the space that lets your team grow and your career move. None of them require you to stop being good at what you do. They require you to stop letting what you're good at be the only thing people see.

***Tool #1: The Guilt / Obligation / Spite Rule.*** Before you take on any task, run it through this filter: Am I doing this out of guilt? Am I doing it out of obligation? Am I doing it out of spite?

If the answer to any of those is yes, it's the wrong motivation and probably the wrong task. Put it down.

I'm serious about the spite one. I've worked with people who were doing work specifically because someone else said they couldn't. Or because a peer tried to take it from them and they dug in out of territorial instinct. That's not strategy. That's ego driving the bus. And ego doesn't take you anywhere useful.

I gave this framework to a client who was agonizing over whether to go above and beyond on a project for a stakeholder who never acknowledged her contributions. "Ask yourself: am I doing this because of guilt, obligation, or spite? If it's any of those, don't do it. Regardless of what the situation might be. Just leave it alone." She decided the answer was obligation, and she stopped. Nothing bad happened. The stakeholder didn't even notice.

**GUILT**
- Say sorry constantly
- Overwork for approval
- Agree to everything

**OBLIGATION**
- Visit family weekly
- Take on extra tasks
- Attend boring events
- Follow old rules

**SPITE**
- Succeed to prove wrong
- Deny affection
- Rebel without purpose

**THE GUILT / OBLIGATION / SPITE TEST**

*Wrong motivation. Right task. Still a problem.*

***Tool #2: The Replaceability Audit.*** List every recurring responsibility you have. For each one, ask two questions: Could someone on my team do this at 70% of my level with coaching? And do I gain anything from doing this other than it getting done?

If you answer yes to the first and no to the second, that's a delegation candidate. Full stop. Even if you enjoy it. Especially if you enjoy it. That enjoyment is the anchor that keeps you at the wrong altitude.

| | TASK/RESPONSIBILITY | ONLY ME? |
|---|---|---|
| | | ☐ |
| | | ☐ |
| | | ☐ |
| | | ☐ |
| | | ☐ |
| | | ☐ |
| | | ☐ |

**THE REPLACEABILITY AUDIT**

*Without me, does it stop?*

***Tool #3: The Visibility Expansion.*** Once you've started to free up capacity from delegation, invest that time in work that expands how people think of you. Volunteer for a cross-functional initiative. Offer a perspective in a meeting that's outside your core domain. Write a point of view on a strategic question. Build a relationship with someone in a different part of the organization.

The goal is to give people a reason to think of you beyond your expertise, so you stop being the dentist. This isn't about abandoning your domain. It's about adding dimensions to how people perceive you. You want them to think, "Marcus is great at client operations, and he also has a really interesting perspective on our go-to-market strategy." That "and" is the difference between being stuck and being considered.

***Tool #4: The Bench Test.*** For your strongest team members, start exposing them to your world. Bring them to meetings they wouldn't normally attend. Let them present work you'd normally present. Give them visibility to your peers and your leadership. Not all at once —

gradually. You're not dumping work. You're expanding their operating altitude. And in doing so, you're building the bench that makes your own advancement possible. Because the day your boss thinks "Who would run Marcus's team?" and there's an obvious answer — that's the day your cage door opens.

**THE CAGE DOOR**

*The door' s been open for a while.*

One caveat: in some organizations, a self-sufficient team gets misread. The leader who's built a team that runs without them looks — to the wrong observer — like a leader who isn't involved enough. If you're in that environment, the fix isn't to re-insert yourself into the work. It's to make the design visible. "My team operates independently because I built it that way" is a very different narrative than "my team operates independently because I'm checked out." Tell the story of the design. The people above you can't read your intent — they can only see your presence. Make sure they understand that your absence from the operational work is evidence of your leadership, not the absence of it.

## THE EXPERIMENT

Let's try two experiments: one immediate, one this month.

This week: pick one task that you normally do yourself — one that gives you that little hit of validation when you do it well — and hand it to someone on your team. Give them the context, set the expectation, and then don't touch it. Let them do it. Even if it's not how you would have done it. Even if you can see the places where you would have done it better.

And here's the part most leaders miss: sometimes they'll do it differently and it will be better. Not despite the fact that they did it their way — because of it. They're closer to the work than you are. They see things you don't. If you let them.

At the end, evaluate: Was the outcome acceptable? If so, that's one thing off your plate permanently. If it wasn't acceptable, that's coaching information — now you know exactly where to develop them. Either way, you learned something. And you didn't do it yourself. That's progress.

This month: identify one meeting or one conversation outside your core domain where you can contribute a perspective. Not a presentation. Not a project. Just a moment where you add value in a space where people don't currently associate with you. Do it once. See how people respond. That response is data about how ready the organization is to see you differently.

## THE MIRROR

- If your team could function without you for a month, would that make you feel relieved or terrified? What does that answer tell you about where your identity is anchored?
- What's the difference between being valued and being needed? Which one are you actually pursuing? Be ruthlessly honest.
- What would your career look like if you made yourself completely replaceable in your current role within the next six months?
- What are you doing out of guilt, obligation, or spite that you could stop doing today? What's actually stopping you from stopping?
- If you were promoted tomorrow, who would struggle the most? That person is your development priority. Are you developing them, or are you doing their work for them?
- When someone brings you a problem, how long does it take before you start solving it? Is it seconds? What if you waited a full minute and just asked questions? What would change?
- If you got promoted tomorrow, who would step into your role? If nobody comes to mind, that's the trap. What would you need to let go of to make room for building that person?

I'll leave you with something one of my clients said to me after we'd spent three sessions on this topic. He'd been the fixer for years. He'd been the person everyone came to. He'd been, in every way that mattered, the dentist.

He said, "I think I've been afraid that if I stop being needed, I'll stop mattering."

I told him what I'll tell you: the leaders who matter most are the ones whose teams don't need them. Not because they're absent or disengaged. But because they built something that works. They developed people. They created systems. They made themselves replaceable, which, paradoxically, is the thing that makes them most promotable.

> ***The leaders who matter most are the ones whose teams don't need them. Not because they're absent — because they built something that works.***

That's the escape route. And it starts with handing off one thing this week.

# PART 2

# LEADING OTHERS

*From Doing the Work to Building the People Who Do*

---

*The single hardest transition in professional life isn't getting promoted. It's letting go. Letting go of the work that made you good. Letting go of the problems you're best at solving. Letting go of the version of leadership that felt like competence. The chapters in this section are about what that transition actually requires — and what gets in the way.*

## CHAPTER FIVE

# THE CONVERSATION YOU'RE AVOIDING

*How to say the hard thing without destroying the relationship*

---

*"I know I need to have this conversation. I've been putting it off for three months."*

**— Every coaching client, at some point**

## THE PATTERN

There is one thing that comes up in almost every coaching engagement, without exception. Somewhere in the conversation – sometimes in session one, sometimes in session eight – the person will describe a situation where they know what needs to happen and they know what needs to be said, but they haven't done it.

A direct report who's underperforming and everyone knows it. A peer who keeps overstepping boundaries. A boss who's making promises they can't keep. A team member who keeps bending the rules they agreed to follow.

The conversation is sitting there. Waiting. Getting heavier every day.

Let me tell you about Annika Lindstrom.

Annika was VP of Engineering at a fintech company – there were about 60 people in her organization, headquartered in New York, with a small team in Berlin that she visited quarterly. She was sharp, organized, and very data driven. Not someone who avoided things. She had a reputation for being direct, for running tight operations, and for getting things done.

She had a senior engineer Tomas. The company was in a critical product launch phase and the entire team had agreed – voluntarily – to work from the office full-time until the release stabilized. No remote work during this period. Everyone nodded. Everyone agreed. It was a team commitment.

Then one Thursday morning, Tomas messaged at quarter to eight: "Hurt my knee at the gym last night. Can't walk well. Working from home." Annika said fine. These things happen.

The following Thursday: same thing. Another gym injury. He said he'd go to the doctor, but Annika predicted to herself that Tomas wouldn't actually go. She was right. When she asked, he said, "Oh, the doctor just told me to rest."

Annika came to me and said, "I don't know what to think about it and how to deal with it."

But she did know. That's the thing. She knew exactly what was going on. What she actually didn't know was how to address it without becoming the police – without turning a trust-based team culture into a surveillance operation. She didn't want to be the person who demands doctor's notes and tracks attendance. But she also couldn't let a pattern establish itself because the rest of the team was watching.

I asked her, "What did you do when it happened the second time?"

"I started writing a message," she said. "Then I deleted it. Then I wrote another one. Then I left it in drafts."

That message was still in her drafts two weeks later. And the pattern was still going.

Here's what was happening under the surface: the rest of Annika's team was watching. They were the ones coming in every day, honoring the commitment they'd all made together. And one of them – maybe more than one – was thinking, "If Tomas gets to work from home on Thursdays, why am I dragging myself to the office?"

This is the piece leaders miss about avoidance. The conversation isn't just between you and the person. It's between you and everyone who's watching.

And the higher you operate, the bigger the audience. At altitude, every conversation you avoid sends a signal about what you're willing to tolerate — and that signal travels further than you think.

And what they're watching for is whether you treat exceptions as exceptions or whether you let them quietly become precedent.

I told Annika, "You had a situation earlier where someone got an exception, and now there are people on your team who think that was precedent. It wasn't. It was an exception. But because you didn't explicitly say that — because you left room for interpretation — people filled in the blanks. And some of them filled it in with, 'I guess the rules are flexible.'"

She said, "So I need to have the conversation with Tomas, and I probably need to have a conversation with the whole team about what the actual expectation is."

"Yes," I said. "Because right now, the only thing worse than the ambiguity is the resentment that's building in the people who are following the rules. And that resentment is going to cost you a lot more than a 10-minute conversation with Tomas."

> ***"The issue isn't that you don't know what to say. The issue is that you're afraid of what saying it will cost."***

Avoidance doesn't always look like silence. Sometimes it looks like a leader who talks around the issue instead of about it.

Let me tell you about Gina Medina.

Gina was a Director of customer success at a retail technology company. She had a direct report — a manager who had been on her team for over a year — who kept submitting work that was, in Gina's words, "nowhere near good enough." Not once. Repeatedly. The pattern was clear: this person would do a first pass that was incomplete, hand it to Gina, and then Gina would either fix it herself or send it back with detailed notes that essentially amounted to doing the thinking for them.

The conversation Gina needed to have was this: "The standard of work you're producing isn't meeting expectations. Here's what I need to see. Here's the timeline. And if it doesn't change, here's what happens next."

But that's not the conversation she was having. Instead, she was having softer versions. "How can I help you improve?" "Let me show you what I'm looking for." "Next time, try to add more detail." Each one was a version of the real conversation with the edges sanded off. And each time, the person heard "mostly fine" instead of "this needs to fundamentally change."

Meanwhile, another team member was doing exceptional work and watching Gina spend her Fridays rescuing the underperformer. That person came to Gina and said, essentially, "Why does she get all this extra support when I'm producing at a higher level with no help?"

Fair question. And it's the question that avoidance always generates. When you avoid the hard conversation with the person who needs it, you're having a different hard conversation with the people who don't — they're just not saying it to your face. Yet.

I pushed Gina on this. "What does your high performer think is happening right now?"

Gina paused. "She probably thinks I don't notice the difference."

"Or worse," I said. "She thinks you notice and you don't care. And that's actually the more dangerous interpretation because it tells her that delivering excellence has no advantage over delivering mediocrity in your organization. Once she believes that, she's gone. Not today. But soon."

That landed. Because Gina cared deeply about her team. The avoidance wasn't about the underperformer — it was about her discomfort with confrontation. And she was paying for that discomfort with the engagement of her best people.

This is the hidden cost of avoidance that most leaders never calculate. The conversation you're not having with the underperformer is creating a conversation the high performer is having with a recruiter.

Every week you wait, the cost compounds.

## THE REFRAME

Here's what I want you to understand about avoidance: every difficult conversation you put off gets harder, not easier. The longer you wait, the more you build it up in your mind, the more the other person's behavior gets reinforced, and the more complicated the eventual conversation becomes. That thing you've been avoiding for three months? It would have been a five-minute conversation in month one. Now it's a 45-minute confrontation with documentation.

The other thing people don't realize: the avoidance itself is visible. Your team can usually tell when you're avoiding something. They might not know what it is, but they can feel the shift in energy, the way you're dancing around something. And that ambiguity is almost always worse than the direct conversation would have been. People start filling the void with their own stories – and as we discussed in Chapter 3, their stories are usually worse than reality.

I told Annika, "Leave no room for interpretation. If you leave a little bit of room, some people will wiggle right into that space and set up shop."

That applies to Tomas. But it applies everywhere. When you give performance feedback that's vague enough to be interpreted as "mostly fine," the person hears "I'm fine." When you set a boundary with caveats and qualifications, the person hears "it's flexible." When you address pattern behavior by saying "I noticed this happened a couple of times" instead of "This pattern needs to stop," the person hears "It's not that serious."

Be clear. Be direct. Be kind.
But do not leave room for creative interpretation.

And here's the part that Gina needed to hear: every time you rescue an underperformer instead of addressing the underperformance, you're not being kind. You're being avoidant. And the person you're actually hurting is the high performer on your team who's watching you reward mediocrity with your time and attention. That person is the one updating their resume.

> ***"Every difficult conversation you put off gets harder, not easier. And the avoidance itself is visible."***

Language is one of the most underrated tools in a leader's toolkit and one of the most practical interventions I use.

Listen to how you talk about your commitments. Do you say "I'll try"? "Hopefully"? "I'll do my best"? "I'm planning to"?

All of that is escape-hatch language. It sounds committed, but it gives you an out.

And here's the problem — when you use that language, you're modeling it for your team. So now everyone is "trying" and "hoping" and "doing their best," and nobody is actually committing to anything.

Replace all of it with **"I will."** Crisp. Clear. No hedge.

"I will have this conversation by Friday." Not "I'll try to get to it." "I will deliver the report by end of day." Not "I'll do my best to get it done." "I will address this with my team." Not "I'm planning to bring it up."

I worked with a leader whose senior leadership team challenged the entire leadership team to create their "I will" statements for the year — not goals, not aspirations, but commitments stated in "I will" language. That single shift changed the texture of every conversation that followed. Because "I will" doesn't give you an out. It creates a record. And when someone on your team says, "I will do X by Friday" and doesn't, the conversation practically writes itself.

One of my clients left a session and immediately started working "I will" statements into her vocabulary. Two weeks later, she told me her team had picked it up on their own. "They started saying it in meetings without me asking," she said. That's culture change. And it started with two words.

This isn't just language. It's accountability architecture.

## THE FRAMEWORK

Hard conversations fail for predictable reasons — and most of them have nothing to do with what you say. They fail because of when you say it, how you frame it, and whether you follow through afterward. I've watched 100s of these conversations go sideways, and the pattern is almost always the same. These tools address all three failure points.

***Tool #1: Red / Yellow / Green Conversations.*** I developed this framework early in my coaching career, and I've used it with more clients than any other tool in this book. I realized I was treating every difficult conversation like it was a five-alarm fire. They're not. Before any difficult conversation, categorize it. Green means low emotional risk — information sharing, routine feedback, quick check-in. Just do it, don't overthink it. Yellow means moderate risk — performance issues, boundary setting, uncomfortable truths. Prepare your three key points, anticipate one likely reaction, and go. Red means high emotional risk — someone's livelihood, a relationship you value deeply, a confrontation with someone more powerful. Prepare thoroughly, write down your points, and anticipate their response. Then, have it in person, never over email. And don't have it when either of you is emotionally activated.

Here's the critical insight: most of the conversations people are avoiding are yellows that they've convinced themselves are reds.

Annika's conversation with Tomas? Yellow. A 10-minute discussion about expectations and patterns. She'd built it into a red in her mind because she was afraid of damaging team trust. Do the categorization clearly. It will almost always feel more manageable than you think.

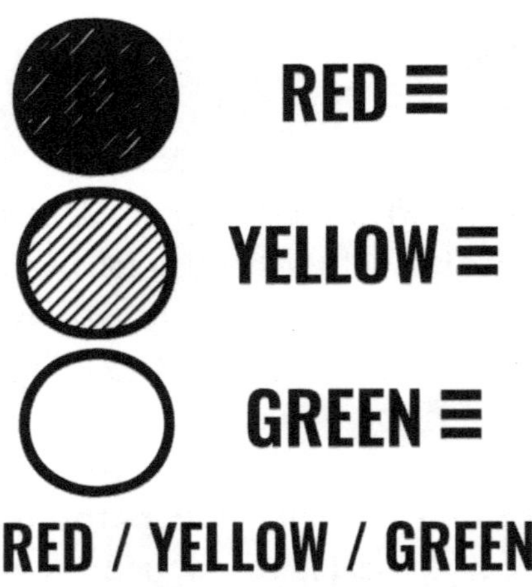


*The yellows are the ones costing you the most.*

***Tool #2: The Closing the Loop Practice.*** When you take action based on someone's feedback, tell them. Explicitly. "We're doing this because of the feedback we heard from you." Don't assume people know why you're doing something. They don't. They gave you feedback six months ago and then watched you do a bunch of things, and they have no idea those things were connected to what they said. Close the loop. It's the most underappreciated leadership skill I see. When people feel heard — not just listened to but heard in a way that produces visible change — they trust you more, give you more honest feedback in the future, and forgive you more readily when things go sideways.

***Tool #3: The 48-Hour Rule.*** If you identify a conversation that needs to happen, schedule it within 48 hours. Not next week. Not when the timing is right. Not after the project wraps up or the quarter ends or the holiday passes. This week. Because the timing will never feel right. There will always be a reason to wait — and those reasons are just the stories you're telling yourself to justify the avoidance. One tactical thing I recommend: when you identify the conversation, immediately open your calendar and send the meeting invite. Before you have time to talk yourself out of it. The act of scheduling it makes it real. Once it's on the calendar, your avoidance has to actively cancel it rather than passively postpone it. That's a much harder thing to justify.

Let me show you what happens when you don't follow the 48-hour rule.

I worked with a director who identified a performance issue with one of his managers in September. He knew the conversation needed to happen. He had the talking points. He even rehearsed them in our coaching session. And then he waited. October came. The quarter was too busy. November came. The holidays were approaching and it felt cruel. January came. "I'll wait until after annual reviews." February. March. By April, the situation had metastasized. The underperforming manager's team had lost two strong contributors who were tired of picking up the slack. The director's own credibility was damaged because his peers had noticed the problem months ago and watched him do nothing.

What would have been a 30-minute conversation in September became a multi-month performance improvement plan in April, followed by a termination in June. Nine months of avoidance produced nine months of organizational damage that didn't need to happen. The director told me afterward, "I spent more time worrying about having the conversation than the conversation would have taken."

That's the math of avoidance. The worry always takes longer than the conversation.

***Tool #4: The Three-Point Prep.*** For any yellow or red conversation, write down exactly three things you want the other person to walk away understanding. Not three pages. Three points. Distill everything into the essential message. If you can't say it in three points, you're not clear enough on what you actually need to communicate. The three-point limit forces precision, and precision is kindness in difficult conversations. People can absorb three things. They cannot absorb a 12-minute monologue about everything that's been bothering you.

**THE CONVERSATION PREP**

*Say the thing you're rehearsing not to say.*

## THE EXPERIMENT

Identify one yellow conversation you've been putting off. Not the scariest one — start with a yellow. Write down the three points you want to make. Next, schedule it within the next 48 hours. Then, have the conversation.

Before you go in, make one decision: Are you using "I will" language or escape-hatch language? Choose "I will." And model it. "I will be more direct about expectations from here." "I will give you feedback in real time instead of saving it." Watch how it changes the tone of the conversation.

Afterward, notice what actually happened versus what you were afraid would happen. In my experience, the gap between those two things is enormous. The conversation you've been dreading for three months usually takes 15 minutes and ends with the other person saying, "Thanks for telling me. I didn't realize."

And you'll wonder why you waited so long. Everyone does.

## THE MIRROR

- What conversation have you been avoiding the longest? What's it costing you to keep avoiding it — not in theory, but in actual energy, actual team trust, and actual results?

- When you commit to something, do you use "I will" or "I'll try"? Listen to yourself for a week. Count the escape hatches. What would change if you eliminated every hedge from your vocabulary?

- What feedback have you received from your team that you never closed the loop on? What message does that silence send?

- Are you avoiding the conversation to protect them, or to protect yourself? Be honest. Most avoidance is self-protection dressed up as consideration.

- What's the worst thing that actually happened the last time you had a difficult conversation? Was it as bad as you feared? And what happened to the relationship afterward?

- Who on your team is watching you avoid a conversation with someone else? What is that teaching them about what's acceptable?

- If you had the conversation tomorrow, what would you wish you'd said? Write it down. That's your script.

- What's the cost of the conversation you're not having? Not the imagined cost of having it — the actual cost of not having it. What's eroding while you wait?

- When you finally had a difficult conversation in the past, did the relationship survive? In most cases, it got stronger. What does that pattern tell you about the one you're avoiding now?

A client said something to me after finally having a conversation she'd been avoiding for four months. It was a performance conversation with a direct report she liked as a person. She'd been protecting the relationship by avoiding the truth.

After the conversation, she called me. "You know what she said? She said, 'I wish you'd told me this months ago. I've been struggling and I didn't know how to bring it up.'"

The person she'd been protecting didn't want to be protected. She wanted to be told the truth. She wanted someone to care enough to be direct. And all those months of avoidance hadn't been kindness. They'd been a mutual silence that was making everything worse.

That's the thing about difficult conversations. They're almost always harder in your imagination than they are in reality. And the person on the other side is almost always more ready to hear the truth than you're giving them credit for.

> ***The conversation you're avoiding is costing you more than the conversation itself ever would.***

Have the conversation. This week. Not perfectly. Just directly.

## CHAPTER SIX

# STOP CATCHING EVERY BALL

*The difference between helping and enabling*

---

*"I know I should let them struggle. But it's so much faster if I just do it myself."*

**— A director who couldn't understand why his team wasn't growing**

## THE PATTERN

In Chapter Four, we looked at the Dentist Trap from the outside — what it costs you when you're too essential to be moved. This chapter is about the same problem from the inside, and the stakes are higher: what it costs your team when you can't stop solving things for them. At director level, doing their work costs you time. At VP level, it costs you talent — because the people who want to grow will leave to find a leader who lets them.

I'll tell you something about myself. Earlier in my career, when I was managing teams, I did the same thing I see my clients doing now. Someone would come to me with a problem, and I would solve it. Quickly, efficiently, completely. And I felt good about that. It felt like leadership.

> ***I was creating codependencies instead of creating independence. It took me a long time to understand the difference.***

I share that because I want you to know this isn't theoretical for me. I've made this mistake. And the version of it I see most often in the leaders I coach isn't negligence or ego — it's the opposite. It's leaders who care deeply about their teams, who want things to go well, who are trying to help. And who have accidentally built teams that can't function without them.

Let me tell you about James Okafor.

James was a director of event operations at a large media company with 20 years in the industry. He knew how everything worked and he was proud of that — rightly so. His team had strong results, clients trusted him, and he was seen as a reliable operator.

That was the problem. He was still handling everything that walked through the door.

His team would bring him problems, and he would listen to fix rather than listen to develop. I want to be specific about what that distinction means because it's the center of this chapter.

**LISTEN TO FIX VS. LISTEN TO DEVELOP**

*The problem moves in opposite directions.*

**When you listen to fix,** you're taking ownership of the problem. You're hearing the situation, and your brain is immediately jumping to solutions. You might ask questions, but those questions are really just your way of getting to the answer faster. The person walks away with a solution — your solution — and no better equipped to solve the next one on their own.

**When you listen to develop,** you're keeping the problem with the person. You're asking questions that help them think through it themselves. You're slower in the moment. And you've just communicated that you believe they can figure it out.

James was a fixer. His team knew it. And they'd learned to bring him everything — not because they couldn't think for themselves, but because they'd been trained out of trying.

I came back to the delegation framework from Chapter One: "You get to set the who, what, where, when, and why. The how is up to them. If you're getting involved in the how, you're below your altitude. And even when they ask you for help with the how, be careful. If you're too prescriptive, they're not learning — you're just creating a more elaborate dependency."

The turning point came when James tried an experiment I gave him. Instead of answering the next question that came his way, he asked, "What would you do if I weren't here?" The person paused, thought about it, and offered an approach that was 80% right. James's instinct was to correct the 20%. Instead, he said, "Run with it."

The person ran with it. The client was fine. The world didn't end. And James had just done the thing that three years of good intentions hadn't accomplished: he'd created a moment where his team member actually developed.

"That was harder than I expected," he told me the next session. "Not the delegation. The sitting on my hands afterward."

> ***That's exactly right. The hard part isn't handing off the work. It's tolerating the discomfort of watching someone else do it differently than you would.***

Here's a version from the other side – from someone who was developing well and nearly got derailed by her own leader.

Let me tell you about Sandra Park.

Sandra was a senior director at a tech company who had a strong team with real potential. One of her managers, in particular, was ready for more. Sandra knew it. And she was doing the right things – giving this person more exposure, letting her present to senior leadership, and expanding her scope gradually.

But Sandra had a habit that was undermining all of it. Every time this manager brought her a recommendation, Sandra would accept it – and then add to it. "That's a great idea. And also, we should probably do X. And have you thought about Y?" Every time. Without fail.

The intent was good. Sandra was trying to make the recommendation better. But the impact was devastating. Her manager started second-guessing every recommendation before bringing it forward because she knew Sandra was going to add to it anyway. The unspoken message was: Your thinking is good, but not good enough. It always needs my improvement.

I asked Sandra, "What would happen if the next time she brought you a recommendation, you just said 'Go'? No additions. No refinements. Just approval."

She was physically uncomfortable with the idea. "But what if she misses something important?"

"Then she'll learn from that," I said. "Which is infinitely more valuable than learning that her boss will always catch what she missed. One builds independence. The other builds learned helplessness."

> ***Sandra's additions weren't fixing problems. They were preventing her best person from developing the confidence to operate without a safety net. And at the level Sandra wanted this person to reach, operating without a safety net is the job.***

## THE REFRAME

I told my own teams something years ago that changed how we worked together. There's an old rule in vampire mythology — a vampire can't enter your home unless you invite them in. They can stand at the door all night. They can see exactly what's happening inside. But they can't cross the threshold without your permission.

I told my team: think of me the same way. I might see a problem you're working through. I might have an opinion about how to solve it. I might even have a better answer than the one you're building. But I'm not going to walk in uninvited. If you want my input, ask for it. If you want me to weigh in on a decision, open the door. But the default is that I stay on my side of the threshold — because the moment I start walking in uninvited, you stop developing the judgment to handle it yourself.

The rule changed two things immediately. First, my team stopped waiting for me to intervene — because they knew I wouldn't. They started solving problems faster, more creatively, and with more ownership. Second, when they did invite me in, the conversations were better — because they'd already done the thinking. They weren't asking me to solve it. They were asking me to pressure-test their solution. That's a completely different conversation.

When you shift from "I'll tell you what to do" to "You have to ask me when you need help," something powerful happens. First, people start trying to solve things on their own before coming to you — because they have to actively make the decision to ask. That decision point is development in itself. Second, when they do come to you, they've usually already thought about it, which means the conversation is richer and more productive. And third, you start to see who on your team actually can't operate independently — which is developmental information you desperately need.

The hardest version of this is watching someone struggle with something you could handle immediately. Every instinct is screaming to jump in. But if they can't do it when you're standing right there, how can you be confident they can do it when you're not? That struggle — that slightly uncomfortable process of working through something without the safety net — is where growth actually happens.

I had to learn this the hard way. And so will most of you. Because the instinct to rescue is deeply satisfying in the moment. It makes you feel capable and needed. But it makes your team weaker every single time you do it.

Your job is not to be the expert who solves everything. Your job is to build a team of people who can solve things without you. Those are not the same job. And you cannot do both at once.

There's a concept I use with every leader I work with that ties this together — adding value versus detracting value.

A senior executive I coached described his leadership philosophy this way: every day, your job is to find things that add value and do more of them, and to find things that detract value — the little bleeds, the inefficiencies, the patterns that are slowly eroding quality — and eliminate them. That's leadership. That's the whole job, distilled.

The problem is that most leaders confuse "adding value" with "doing the work." They think they're adding value when they jump in and solve a problem. And in the immediate moment, they are. The problem gets solved. But they're simultaneously detracting value from their team's development. And over time, the detracting compounds faster than the adding.

> ***Every time you solve a problem your team could have solved, you've added value to the moment and detracted value from the system. The net is negative. Even though it doesn't feel that way when you're doing it.***

I asked one of my clients to track this for a week. Every time he intervened on something his team was handling, he marked whether it was adding or detracting value to the system. At the end of the week, he was surprised — and a little shaken. Roughly 60 percent of his interventions were detracting. They made the immediate outcome slightly better while teaching his team that the boss would always be there to polish things.

"The worst part," he said, "is that most of my additions were marginal. I was improving things from a B-plus to an A-minus. And the cost was my team never learning to get to an A-minus on their own."

I worked with a director who ran a team of 12 and couldn't understand why none of them were ready for promotion. She was talented, dedicated, and involved in every decision her team made. That was the problem. Her involvement was so constant that her team had never developed the judgment muscles that promotion requires. They could execute beautifully — as long as she was there to shape the execution. The moment she stepped away, quality dropped. Not because they lacked ability. Because they'd never been allowed to fail at the level where real learning happens.

I asked her to try something for one month: pick two decisions per week that she would normally make herself, and hand them to her team instead. Not delegate the task — delegate the decision. Let them choose the approach, live with the outcome, and learn from it. She was miserable the first week. "They're going to do it wrong," she told me. Some of them did. And those mistakes taught more in a month than her corrections had taught in a year. By week four, two of her people were making decisions she hadn't anticipated — better decisions than she would have made, because they were closer to the work than she was.

> ***Your team's ceiling is set by how much space you give them to fail. If you're filling all the space, they'll never outgrow you — and you'll never outgrow this role.***

That's the math that most leaders never do. The marginal improvement you add by intervening versus the developmental opportunity you subtract by not letting them figure it out. When you actually calculate it, the math almost always favors letting go.

## THE FRAMEWORK

Developing people is the hardest thing most leaders do — not because it's complicated, but because it requires you to do less. Every tool here is designed to shift your default from solving to developing. They won't feel natural at first. That discomfort is the point — it means you're building a new muscle instead of relying on the old one.

***Tool #1: The Listen-to-Develop Switch.*** Before your next one-on-one, decide in advance: I am not going to solve anything in this meeting. My only job is to ask questions that help this person solve it themselves. The two questions that work in almost every situation: "What have you already considered?" and "What would you do if I weren't here?" Then stop talking.

***Tool #2: The Vampire Rule.*** Establish an explicit norm with your team: they have to invite you in. You will not insert yourself into their work uninvited. If they want your opinion, they ask. If they want direction, they ask. If they don't ask, you trust that they're handling it. That one shift changes the entire dynamic from dependency to ownership.

**THE VAMPIRE RULE**

*They have to invite you in.*

***Tool #3: The Add / Detract Audit.*** For one week, every time you intervene in something your team is handling, mark it. At the end of the week, assess: Was the outcome meaningfully better? Or were you improving things from a B-plus to an A-minus while costing someone a development opportunity? Most leaders find the ratio is not what they expected.

***Tool #4: The Refinement Pause.*** The next time someone brings you a recommendation and your instinct is to improve it, pause first. Ask yourself two questions: Is this refinement necessary, or is it just better? Then ask, What am I communicating to this person by making it? Sometimes the refinement is actually necessary. Often it isn't. The pause lets you choose.

## THE EXPERIMENT

In your next one-on-one, when someone brings you a problem, don't solve it. Ask two questions: "What have you considered so far?" and "What would you do if I weren't here?" Then let them answer. Resist every urge to correct, improve, or add. If their approach is 70% right, let them run with it. 70 percent with ownership is worth infinitely more than 100% that came from you.

Then observe: What happened? Did the sky fall? Or did they surprise you?

My prediction: they'll surprise you. They almost always do. The capability was there all along. It just never had room to show up because you were filling all the space.

And here's the second experiment: run the Add / Detract Audit this week. Every time you intervene on something your team is handling, mark it. Don't solve what you flag. Just observe. Take notes. Let them own the work.

By the end of the week, you'll have a development map for your entire team that you didn't have to create yourself. They created it for you. That's how development works when you get out of the way.

## THE MIRROR

- When someone on your team brings you a problem, is your first instinct to solve it or to develop them? Be honest about the ratio. If it's 80/20 in favor of solving, that's the number you need to flip.

- How much of your involvement in your team's work is because they need you versus because you need to feel useful? Sit with that question. It's the one most leaders don't want to answer.

- If you took a two-week vacation tomorrow with no email access, what would break? That's your development priority list. Everything that would break is something you haven't built the capability around.

- Who on your team is closest to being ready to take on more? What's one thing you could give them this month to accelerate that readiness?

- When's the last time someone on your team solved a significant problem without involving you at all? If you can't think of an example, what does that tell you?

- What would change if you told your team: "From now on, don't bring me problems — bring me your proposed solution and we'll discuss it." What would you gain? What would you lose? Which matters more?

- Are you building a team that needs you or a team that chooses you? There's a profound difference. And only one of them survives your next promotion.

I'll leave you with something I tell every leader I work with on this topic.

The goal is not to make yourself unnecessary. That's a fear that keeps a lot of leaders holding on too tightly. The goal is to make yourself unnecessary at the level you're at so that you become available at the level above. Your team doesn't need you less. They need you differently. They need you as a coach, as a strategist, as a connector, as someone who opens doors. Not as the person who reviews their spreadsheets.

> ***When you let go of being the expert who solves, you make room to become the leader who builds. Not in the problems you solved today. In the people you developed who will solve tomorrow's problems without you. That's a legacy. Everything else is just activity.***

# PART 3

# THE ORGANIZATIONAL GAME

*Navigating the Reality Nobody Teaches You*

---

*Being good at your job is necessary but not sufficient. Careers are shaped as much by visibility, relationships, and organizational awareness as by performance. The chapters in this section are about the game that runs underneath the work — and how to navigate it without becoming someone you don't recognize.*

## CHAPTER SEVEN

# MANAGING UP WITHOUT SELLING OUT

*How to advocate for yourself without becoming the person you hate*

---

*"I just want to do good work and have it speak for itself. Is that too much to ask?"*

**— Yes. Unfortunately, yes.**

## THE PATTERN

Every time I hear someone say, "I'm not political," I brace myself. Because what they usually mean is, "I haven't learned to navigate the organization, and I'm paying for it."

I see this pattern in at least half my coaching engagements. Someone with real talent, real results, and zero visibility. They're doing excellent work and assuming the work will speak for itself. It won't. It never does. Not at this altitude. The work that speaks for itself is the work that gets done by someone else while you get credit for managing the perception. That's not cynicism — that's how organizations actually function above a certain level. And the sooner you recognize it, the sooner you can start playing the game on your terms instead of pretending it doesn't exist.

Let me tell you about Priya Sharma.

Priya was a senior director of analytics at a professional services firm. She'd been in the role for four years. She ran a team of 22 people. She'd built the analytics practice from scratch, created frameworks that were now used firm-wide, and consistently delivered results that exceeded expectations. By any objective measure, she was one of the highest-performing leaders in her division.

And her boss barely knew she existed.

I don't mean that literally. He knew her name. He attended her quarterly reviews. He signed off on her budget. But when it came to the informal influence that shapes careers — the hallway conversations, the mentions in leadership meetings, the recommendations for high-visibility projects — Priya was invisible.

She told me, "I have no clue where I stand, what he thinks about my performance, if he even notices anything I do."

Here's the brutal irony: Priya was an expert in engagement research. She knew the Gallup data cold. She taught workshops on the finding that being ignored creates more disengagement than being criticized. Being told you're doing a bad job is painful. Being told nothing at all is devastating. The research she taught other leaders was describing her own experience. She was living the case study.

When I pointed this out, she laughed — the kind of laugh that isn't really a laugh. "Yes. I'm the case study."

But here's the part Priya didn't want to hear: her boss wasn't ignoring her on purpose. He had 40 direct and indirect reports, a board that was demanding quarterly results, and a merger integration that was consuming 80% of his bandwidth. Priya wasn't being punished. She was being deprioritized. And the reason she was being deprioritized was that she'd never given him a reason to prioritize her. She did her work, delivered her results, and waited for recognition to come to her.

I asked her, "When was the last time you proactively told your boss about something your team accomplished?"

Silence.

"When was the last time you framed a project in terms of his priorities instead of your workstream?"

More silence.

"When was the last time you had a conversation with him that wasn't about a problem you needed him to solve?"

She looked at me and said, "I see where this is going."

"You're not invisible because he's a bad boss," I said. "You're invisible because you've been treating visibility like it's his responsibility. It's not. It's yours."

The visibility wasn't going to happen on its own.

And here's the thing that's uncomfortable to say but needs to be said: Priya's boss wasn't the only problem. She had colleagues who were doing objectively less visible work but who were far more present in the room. They sent updates. They framed their projects in the language of organizational priorities. They built relationships with people outside their direct reporting line. Priya looked at all of that and thought, "That's political. I'm not going to play that game."

But they weren't playing a game. Most of them were simply communicating. They were keeping their stakeholders informed. They were framing their work so that people with competing demands could quickly understand why it mattered. That's not politics. That's professional competence at senior levels.

Priya had conflated communication with self-promotion. And that conflation was costing her everything she'd worked for.

> ***Your boss isn't ignoring you on purpose. They're just not thinking about you. That's your problem to solve, not theirs.***

Priya's version is about invisibility. But this chapter isn't just for people who are invisible. It's also for people who are watching someone else play the game and feeling sick about it.

Let me tell you about Martin Hayes.

Martin was a VP at a technology company, and he had a peer — a woman who spent, in his estimation, 80% of her time managing up and 20% actually leading her team. She was skilled at it. She positioned herself as the protector, the bulldog, the person getting things done. The people above her saw a completely different picture than the people below her.

Martin found this infuriating. He told me, "She doesn't care about the wake behind her. She only focuses on how things look to the people above."

And he wasn't wrong. There are people who manage up in ways that are destructive — who throw colleagues under the bus, who take credit for others' work, who compartmentalize their teams to prevent information from flowing freely. Those people exist. And they often get promoted faster than you'd like, precisely because they're skilled at managing perception.

But here's what I told Martin: "You're watching someone do it badly and using that as a reason to not do it at all. Those are not your only two options."

There is a version of managing up that is ethical, honest, and necessary. It doesn't involve manipulation or self-promotion. It involves communication. And the failure to do it isn't principled. It's self-sabotaging.

## THE REFRAME

Managing up is not manipulation. It's not kissing up, playing games, or compromising your integrity. Here's the reframe I offer most often: it's not bragging if it's keeping stakeholders informed.

Your boss has dozens — maybe 100s — of things competing for their attention. If you're not surfacing your work, your priorities, and your wins in a way that's easy for them to consume, they're not going to go looking for them. That's not malice. That's not indifference. That's capacity.

I worked with a director who was preparing a roadmap presentation for a new executive. She was going to send the entire thing — 30 slides covering every initiative across every workstream. I pushed back.

"What were the four things she was most interested in when you talked to her?" I asked.

She listed them.

"Lead with those. Frame your work in terms of what she already told you she cares about. Then provide the full picture for context. If all she reads is those four things, that's a win."

That's managing up. It's not gaming the system. It's respecting how the system works. Your boss doesn't need your 30 slides. They need your four most relevant points, framed in their language and connected to their priorities. Everything else is noise — well-intentioned noise, but noise nonetheless.

> ***It's not bragging. It's keeping stakeholders informed. And it's literally your job.***

There's another piece of this: what I call back-channel awareness. In most organizations, the real conversations happen behind closed doors. Decisions get shaped in one-on-one meetings that aren't on anyone's calendar. Reputations get built or damaged in hallway conversations you're not part of.

Pretending this doesn't happen doesn't make you principled. It makes you uninformed. I've worked with leaders who were shocked to learn that conversations about their performance were happening in rooms they didn't even know existed. They felt betrayed. But it wasn't betrayal — it was organizational reality. And the leaders who thrive are the ones who are aware of that reality, even if they don't participate in it the way the political operators do.

**THE POLICE CAR**

***Everyone drives differently when they know they're being watched.***

I'm not saying you have to become a political operator. I'm saying you have to be aware of the political landscape. Know where the conversations are happening. Build relationships with people who have visibility into how decisions get made. Not so you can manipulate the system — so you can navigate it without getting blindsided.

Martin eventually came around to this. His breakthrough happened when he realized that his refusal to manage up wasn't principled neutrality — it was passive protest. He was so frustrated by watching his peer do it badly that he'd sworn off the entire practice. "It's like watching someone use a hammer badly and then refusing to ever use a hammer," I told him. "The hammer isn't the problem. The person using it is."

Once he separated the skill from the person he'd been watching abuse it, everything shifted. He started having deliberate conversations with his boss about priorities. He started framing his team's work in terms of organizational impact, not just execution. He started building relationships with peers in other functions. And none of it required him to throw anyone under the bus or compromise his values. It just required him to communicate.

Six months later, his boss promoted him to a cross-functional leadership role. The peer who spent 80% of her time managing up? She was still in the same position. Because at some point, managing up without delivering catches up with you. But delivering without managing up will also leave you stuck. You need both.

## THE FRAMEWORK

Nobody teaches this stuff. Not in MBA programs, not in leadership development, not in the thousand books about managing up. But managing up — making your work visible, framing it in the language your leadership actually cares about, building the relationships that carry your name into rooms you're not in — that's where careers stall or accelerate. These four tools are what I wish someone had given me 20 years ago.

***Tool #1: The Strategic Narrative.*** Before any interaction with senior leadership, ask yourself one question: What do they care about most right now? Then frame everything you say in those terms. Not your roadmap. Their priorities. The work doesn't change. The framing does. If your boss cares about cost reduction and you're presenting a new initiative, lead with the cost impact — not the innovation. If they're worried about retention, frame your team's work in terms of its impact on keeping people. Same work. Different frame. But the right frame is the difference between your boss leaning in and your boss checking their phone.

***Tool #2: The Friday Update.*** If you only do one thing from this chapter, do this. Send your boss a brief end-of-week update. Three bullets: what you accomplished this week, what's in progress, and one thing you need from them. Do it for four consecutive weeks. It takes you five minutes and it changes your visibility.

I know what you're thinking: that feels like bragging. It's not bragging. It's communication. And communication is your job. When Priya started doing this, the shift was almost immediate. Her boss started referencing her updates in his own leadership meetings. Not because she asked him to. Because she'd made it easy for him to talk about her work. She'd done the framing for him.

Here's the nuance that matters: the Friday update isn't about you. It's about giving your boss what they need to advocate for your team in the rooms you're not in. When your boss walks into a leadership meeting and someone asks, "What's happening in Priya's group?" you want your boss to have an answer that sounds informed and confident. If they don't have one, they either wing it — which is never good for you — or they deflect, which signals that your work isn't top of mind. The Friday update solves both problems. You're not promoting yourself. You're arming your sponsor.

I'll tell you what changed for Priya over the course of several months. She started the Friday updates. She started framing her work in terms of her boss's priorities. She started having deliberate conversations with peers in other functions. None of it was dramatic. None of it required her to become someone she wasn't. It was incremental, consistent communication.

And then one day she came to a session and said, "He mentioned me in the all-hands. By name. He talked about what my team accomplished." She was shocked. I wasn't. Because she'd finally given him the material to work with. He'd always been willing to advocate for her. He just hadn't known what to say.

***Tool #3: The Sponsor Map.*** A mentor gives advice. A coach helps you find answers. A sponsor puts their name next to yours in rooms you're not in. You need all three, but sponsors move careers.

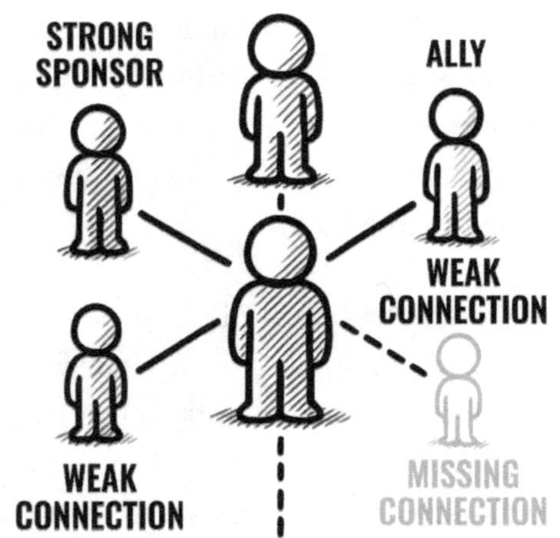

Here's what I see clients get wrong about sponsorship every time: they think they need to find a sponsor and then ask them to be one. That's backwards. Sponsorship is earned, not requested. You earn it by doing excellent work that's visible to the right people, by being reliable when they need something, and by making their life easier in some concrete way. Over time, they start advocating for you not because you asked, but because your work speaks through them.

I tell my clients to identify three to five people in their organization who have influence over the decisions that matter for their career — promotions, high-visibility projects, budget allocation, organizational design. Then ask: Do these people know what I'm working on? Have I made their life easier recently? Would they describe me as someone they'd put their name behind? If the answer to any of those is no, that's your next investment.

Martin's turning point came partly from this. Once he stopped boycotting the entire concept of managing up, he realized he had two natural sponsors he'd been ignoring — senior leaders who already respected his work but who he'd never given material to work with. He started sharing wins with them. He started asking for their input on strategic decisions. He started making himself useful to them in ways that went beyond his direct responsibilities. Within six months, both of them were advocating for him in leadership discussions he didn't even know were happening.

***Tool #4: The Perception Audit.*** Ask three people you trust — a peer, a direct report, and someone more senior — to describe your reputation in one sentence. Don't explain or defend what they say. Just listen. The gap between how you see yourself and how others see you is your managing-up development area. If they describe you as "great executor" and you want to be seen as a "strategic leader," that gap is your priority.

## THE EXPERIMENT

This week, find out your boss's top three priorities. Not what you think they are — what they actually are. Ask directly if you need to: "What's keeping you up at night this quarter?" Then look at your work and ask: How much of what I'm doing connects to those three things? Where is there a gap?

If you can't connect your work to their priorities in one sentence each, you have a framing problem. And framing problems are visibility problems in disguise.

Then send your first Friday update. Three bullets. Five minutes. Watch what happens.

Here's what to put in it: one thing you accomplished this week, one thing you're working on next week, and one thing where you could use input or support. That's it. No preamble, no apology for sending it, no lengthy context. Just signal. Most people who start this practice tell me the same thing after a month: "My boss started responding to them." That response is the beginning of a different relationship — one where your work is visible and your judgment is trusted. You built that with five minutes on a Friday.

## THE MIRROR

Be honest with these. They're harder than they look.

- When's the last time you proactively told your boss about a win? Not forwarded a compliment from a client — told them directly. If you're drawing a blank, that's worth sitting with.

- Do you know what your boss's top three priorities are right now? Not your guess — their actual priorities. Can you connect your work to them in one sentence each?

- Is your resistance to "managing up" about principle, or is it about discomfort with self-promotion? Those are very different things. And only one of them is serving you.

- Who in your organization has the influence to advocate for you? Do they know what you're working on? Have you given them material to work with?

- If your boss were asked right now to describe your top three contributions this year, could they? If not, whose fault is that?

- Are you letting someone else's bad behavior be your excuse for not doing the healthy version of the same thing?

## CHAPTER EIGHT

# EXECUTIVE PRESENCE IS NOT WHAT YOU THINK

*It's not about being louder. It's about being intentional.*

---

*"I need to work on my executive presence. But I'm not even sure what that means."*

**— Nearly every coaching client, at some point**

## THE PATTERN

Executive presence is the single most common development goal people bring to coaching. And almost nobody can define it.

Some think it means being confident. Others think it means being polished. Some think it's about how you speak. Others think it's about how you look. I've had people tell me they need executive presence when what they actually need is to speak up in meetings. I've had people tell me they need it when what they actually need is to stop over-explaining.

Here's what I've learned from working with 100s of professionals on this: executive presence is intentional impact. It's the gap between how you show up and how people experience you. And closing that gap requires awareness, not personality change. That's the conversation I have with clients — not "be more confident," but "be more deliberate."

Let me tell you about Elena Torres.

Elena was a VP at a pharmaceutical company. She'd been hired from a competitor where the culture was very direct — the kind of place where challenge was welcome, debate was the currency, and you'd say things like "I'm going to play devil's advocate here" and everyone would lean in.

Elena's first three months at the new company were a slow collision between who she was and what the culture expected.

The first time she said "I'm going to play devil's advocate," her colleagues pulled her aside after the meeting. "Please don't say things like that," they told her. "When you frame yourself as the adversary, people just hear the adversary part. If you have something to say, just say it. But don't set yourself up as the opposition before you've even made your point."

"I say that all the time," she told me. "It's just how we talked at my last company."

"That's the point," I said. "You're operating with cultural assumptions from a different place. The substance of what you're saying is probably right. But the framing is undermining the substance."

She adapted. She learned to say "I want to explore a different angle on this" instead of "let me play devil's advocate." Same contribution. Completely different reception. The insight didn't change. The packaging did. And in a culture where packaging matters — which, let's be honest, is most cultures — that's the difference between being heard and being tuned out.

The deeper lesson here isn't about word choice. It's about cultural calibration. Elena's presence was fine for her previous environment. It was actively counterproductive in her new one. And she had no idea. She thought she was being rigorous. Her colleagues heard adversarial. The gap between her intent and their experience — that gap is where executive presence lives.

I told her, "You don't have a presence problem. You have a translation problem. The substance is there. We just need to deliver it in the language this culture speaks."

She worked on it deliberately over several months. She started noticing how the most respected leaders in her new organization made their points — with questions instead of challenges, with curiosity instead of opposition, with "Help me understand" instead of "I disagree." None of them were less rigorous than Elena. They just packaged the rigor differently. And once she adopted the same approach, people started describing her as "thoughtful and strategic" instead of "difficult." Same person. Same brain. Different reception.

> ***Executive presence is not a personality trait. It's a practice. And the practice can be learned.***

Managing up, which we covered in the last chapter, is about whether people know what you're doing. That's a visibility problem. Presence is different — it's about whether they feel your weight in the room when you're there. Visibility gets you considered. Presence gets you chosen. Those are different problems with different solutions. The next story is about the second one.

Let me tell you about Mei-Lin Carter.

Mei-Lin was a senior director at a consulting firm navigating a major transition — her firm was merging with a UK-based company, and the partners from the acquiring firm were going to be in her offices for a series of meetings that would shape the new organization's direction. This was her chance to be seen by the people who would determine her future in the combined entity.

Mei-Lin was sharp, strategic, and substantive. But she was quiet. Not because she had nothing to say — because she was calculating whether what she had to say was good enough. Sound familiar? We talked about this pattern in Chapter 2. But here, the solution wasn't about overcoming the imposter. It was about being strategic with presence.

For the big meeting, she did two things that were small but deliberate. First, she planned one specific contribution that would uplift the conversation without putting the spotlight squarely on herself — a synthesis of a key data point that she knew nobody else in the room would have. Second, she wore a bright red blazer in a room full of navy and charcoal.

The blazer might sound trivial. It wasn't. It was a deliberate choice to be memorable in a room of people she was meeting for the first time. She wanted them to leave thinking, "Who was the woman in red who made that observation about the client data?"

That's executive presence. Not the blazer itself — the intentionality behind it. She walked in with a plan for what she would contribute and a decision about how she would be remembered. Most people walk into those meetings hoping to survive them. Mei-Lin walked in with a strategy. That's the difference.

What happened after was even more instructive. In the weeks following that meeting, two of the UK partners reached out to Mei-Lin directly. They remembered her. Not because of the blazer — because of the data point she'd contributed. But the blazer made her findable. She was the woman in red who said the smart thing. Both pieces mattered.

> ***This is the part about presence that most people get wrong: they think it's about one big moment. It's not. It's about the accumulation of small, deliberate choices.***

I've worked with professionals at every level on this, and the ones who develop the strongest presence all share one quality: they think about how they show up before they show up. They don't wing it and hope for the best. They make deliberate decisions about what they'll contribute, when they'll contribute it, and how they want people to experience them. It takes about five minutes of preparation. And it changes everything.

Executive presence is how the organization reads your altitude. It's the signal that tells people whether you're operating at your level or still performing at the one below it.

## THE REFRAME

Here's a framework for presence that I think is more useful than anything you'll read in a corporate training program.

**Composure under pressure**. Can you stay steady when the room gets heated? Can you be the person who slows things down rather than speeds them up when emotions are running high? I ask every client this, and most of them pause before answering — which tells me everything. Early in my career, I was the person who matched the energy. If the room was tense, I got tense. If someone was frustrated, I absorbed it. It took me years to learn that the most powerful thing a leader can do in a heated moment is not match the energy. I started calling this being the thermostat, not the thermometer. You want to set the temperature in the room, not just react to whatever's happening.

I use this analogy often because it captures something essential about leadership presence. When things get tense, the person who stays composed and redirects — that person has presence. The person who matches the energy and escalates — they're just a thermometer. They're reading the room and reflecting it back. That's not leadership. That's reactivity.

One of my clients put it beautifully: "It's not about being fake. I'm such an honest person that I struggle to put up my own walls. But being the thermostat doesn't mean being dishonest. It means being intentional about the energy I bring into the room instead of being at the mercy of whatever energy is already there."

I told her, "You can still name what's going on without jumping in the pool. You can say, 'I can see this is getting heated — let's step back and look at what we're actually trying to solve.' That's honest. That's authentic. And it's thermostat behavior — you're resetting the temperature without pretending the heat doesn't exist."

The leaders who do this well have practiced it so many times that it looks effortless. But it's not effortless. It's a skill they built, one heated meeting at a time. And you can build it too — I've watched clients transform on this in a matter of weeks. The first few times you consciously choose to lower the temperature instead of matching it, it's going to feel unnatural. You're going to want to react. Let that urge pass. Slow down. Ask a question. Summarize what you're hearing. Watch what happens to the room. It changes. Every time.

**Clarity of communication**. Can you make your point in 30 seconds? I time my clients on this. Most can't. They over-explain, they caveat, they provide too much context, and by the time they get to the point, the room has moved on. Precision is presence. If you can't say it in 30 seconds, you don't know it well enough yet.

I worked with a director who was brilliant — one of the sharpest analytical minds I've coached. But he would take three minutes to make a point that needed 30 seconds. He'd give the background, the method, the caveats, the exceptions, and then — finally — the conclusion. By then, the senior leaders in the room had stopped listening. They'd already formed their own conclusions and moved on.

I told him, "Lead with the conclusion. Then stop. If they want the background, they'll ask. And here's the thing — they almost never ask.

Because senior leaders don't need to understand how you got there. They need to know where you landed. The how is for your team. The what is for the room."

He resisted. "But if I don't show the work, how will they know it's rigorous?" I told him, "They hired you because you're rigorous. What they need is someone who can distill complexity into clarity. That's the signal at your level."

**Confidence without arrogance**. Can you hold a position without dismissing the people who disagree? This is the one my clients struggle with most. There's a fine line between conviction and stubbornness, and the best leaders walk it by being firm in their perspective while remaining curious about other viewpoints. Elena's old style — devil's advocate — was all conviction, no curiosity. Her new style kept the conviction but added the openness. Same strength, different expression.

**Strategic framing**. Can you connect the detail to the bigger picture? When you speak, do people hear tactics or do they hear strategy? I ask clients to listen to themselves in their next meeting and answer that question. The ability to zoom out — to connect what's happening in the moment to what it means for the organization — is one of the strongest signals of leadership readiness.

**Intentional visibility**. Are you showing up where it matters, or just where it's comfortable? I want you to think about last week. Which meetings did you choose to attend versus which ones you attended because they were on your calendar? Presence isn't something you perform in the moment. It's the accumulated result of 100s of small, intentional decisions.

## THE FRAMEWORK

I'm going to give you four tools. And I want to be clear about what they are — they're practices, not personality traits. You don't need to become a different person. You need to do a few specific things differently. Starting this week. Not "command the room" — that's not advice, that's a fortune cookie.

***Tool #1: The Thermostat Practice.*** This is the presence tool I come back to more than any other. In your next meeting where things get tense, make a conscious choice to lower the temperature. Slow your speaking pace. Ask a clarifying question. Offer a synthesis: "What I'm hearing is..." The person who can redirect a heated room without matching the energy — that person gets noticed. Every single time. Practice this deliberately until it becomes instinct.

**THE THERMOSTAT**

*Are you setting the temperature or reading it?*

Let me give you specific language for this because the concept is easy to understand and hard to execute in the moment. When things get heated, try one of these three phrases: “Let me make sure I understand what we’re actually debating here.” That forces the room to articulate the real disagreement, which is often different from what people are arguing about. Or: “It sounds like we agree on the goal but disagree on the approach. Can we separate those?” That reframes conflict as alignment, which immediately lowers the temperature. Or simply: “What would need to be true for us both to be right?” That moves the conversation from adversarial to collaborative in one sentence.

Thermostat language doesn’t suppress conflict. It redirects energy from heat to light — if someone has the presence to redirect it. That person should be you.

***Tool #2: The 30-Second Prep.*** Before any meeting with senior leadership, prepare your key message in 30 seconds or less. Write it down. Say it out loud. If you need more than 30 seconds to make your point, you’re not clear enough on what your point actually is. Cut the context, cut the caveats, lead with the conclusion. The context is available if they ask for it. They usually don’t.

***Tool #3: The Bookend Strategy.*** People remember how things start and how things end far more than they remember the middle. Arrive early to important meetings. Make one intentional contribution in the first 10 minutes — this establishes your presence when attention is highest. Then, at the end, offer a brief synthesis or a forward-looking observation. Bookend the meeting with presence and you’ll change how people experience you — even if you’re relatively quiet in the middle.

I developed this advice after watching a pattern across dozens of clients. The ones who were perceived as having strong presence weren’t necessarily the ones who spoke the most. They were the ones who spoke at the right moments. Beginning and end. Those are the moments that stick. Everything in the middle blurs together in people's memory. So if you're going to invest your presence capital, invest it where it compounds.

I had a client who was quiet by nature and found the bookend strategy liberating — it gave her permission to be quiet in the middle. She just had to show up strong in the first 10 minutes and close strong at the end. Within a month, her boss noticed a shift. "You seem more engaged," he said. She was actually speaking less than before. But more strategically.

**THE BOOKEND**

*How you close it matters as much as how you started it.*

***Tool #4: The Three-Word Audit.*** Ask one trusted colleague: "If you had to describe my presence in meetings in three words, what would they be?" Listen to the answer. Don't defend. Don't explain. Just listen. The gap between their perception and your intention is your development area. If you're going for "strategic and composed" and they say "quiet and thorough," that tells you everything about where to focus.

## THE EXPERIMENT

This week, pick one meeting — ideally one with people more senior than you. Do three things: arrive five minutes early and connect with someone informally before it starts, make one substantive contribution in the first 10 minutes, and offer a brief synthesis at the end. Notice how it changes the way people engage with you during and after the meeting.

Then do the three-word audit. Ask someone you trust. One question. Three words. The answer will tell you more about your executive presence than any training program ever could.

One more thing: after the meeting, write down what you contributed and when. Not to grade yourself — to build awareness. Most people have no idea how they actually show up because they've never tracked it. You'll start to see your own patterns — where you go quiet, where you over-explain, where you land. That awareness is the raw material for every presence improvement you'll ever make. You can't change what you can't see.

## THE MIRROR

- Think about these carefully. They're about perception, which means the answers require honesty about how others see you, not how you see yourself.
- If three colleagues described your presence in meetings, what would they say? Would it match what you're going for?

- Are you the thermostat or the thermometer when things get heated? When was the last time you deliberately chose to lower the temperature in a room?
- What's one small, deliberate choice you could make tomorrow about how you show up that would change how people remember you?
- Where are you over-explaining when you could be precise? What would your message sound like in 30 seconds?
- When's the last time you made a deliberate choice about your visibility — not just showed up where you were expected, but chose to be somewhere strategic?
- What cultural assumptions are you carrying from a previous role or company that might be working against you in your current environment?

Executive presence is not something you either have or you don't. That framing has done enormous damage because it makes people think it's a fixed trait — like height or eye color — when it's actually a set of learnable behaviors practiced with intention.

You don't need to be louder. You need to be intentional about the version of yourself you bring into the room. That's it.

**THE LIGHTHOUSE**

*Visible. Consistent. Not chasing the ships.*

## CHAPTER NINE

# SURVIVING THE REORG

*How to lead through chaos, change, and the things you can't control*

---

*"Over the last 48 hours we had a massive reorg. And this one's big — more like three years ago in scale."*

**— A GM, opening what turned out to be one of his most important coaching sessions**

## THE PATTERN

Nearly a third of all my coaching sessions have taken place against some form of organizational disruption — restructuring, RIFs, mergers, acquisitions, leadership transitions. And here's what nobody will tell you directly: a reorg is not just an organizational redesign. It's a political event. The leaders who treat it purely as a "manage through change" exercise while ignoring the positioning game are the ones who wake up in a worse role on the other side.

And yet nobody teaches leaders how to lead through it well. There are books on the topic, but most of them oversimplify the reality — as if change is a four-step process instead of a sustained exercise in holding things together when the ground is moving under everyone's feet, including yours. That's the conversation I have more than any other — not "how do I get better at my job," but "how do I stay steady when everything around me is being reshuffled simultaneously and my team is looking at me to be the calm in the middle of it."

> ***Change is not the exception in professional life. It's the weather. It's not something that happens to you occasionally — it's the environment you operate in every day.***

Let me tell you about Nathan Cole.

Nathan was a General Manager at an enterprise software company — big organization, thousands of employees, the kind of place where reorgs happen annually and people joke darkly about "reorg season." Nathan had a career built on walking into dysfunctional situations and making them work, and an energy for chaos that most people found either inspiring or exhausting.

The week we spoke, Nathan's company had announced a massive restructuring. 100s of people affected. New reporting structures. Eliminated positions. The scale was comparable to a reorg they'd done three years prior — one that had fundamentally reshuffled the entire organization. And it had landed on a Monday morning with about 48 hours of warning.

Nathan's immediate instinct was to over-communicate. "We're trying to move people from ambiguity, concern, question, and doubt back to execution," he told me. "That's the state we're in. Everyone's frozen."

At the same time, he was dealing with a peer who spent most of her time managing up, was "quite political" in his words, and had a philosophy he described as: "What's mine is mine, and what's yours is also mine." She was using the chaos of the reorg as cover to expand her territory. While everyone else was stabilizing their teams, she was grabbing turf.

This is what change actually looks like when you're in the middle of it. It's not one thing. It's everything at once. The organizational disruption. The interpersonal dynamics. The team morale. Your own career uncertainty. And you're supposed to be the calm, steady presence for everyone around you while privately wondering what it all means for your own future.

Nathan told me something that stuck: "Everyone's frozen. My team is looking at me to tell them it's going to be okay, and I don't know if it is. Some of these people are going to lose their jobs. I can't promise them otherwise. But I also can't let the whole organization grind to a halt because everyone's afraid."

That tension — between honesty and reassurance, between transparency and stability — is the central challenge of leading through change. And most leadership advice gets it wrong by telling you to pick a side. "Be transparent!" they say, as if telling your team everything you know will somehow make the anxiety disappear. Or "Stay positive!" as if forced optimism doesn't make people trust you less.

I tell every client the same thing: it's both, held in tension. You can say, "Here's what I know. Here's what I don't know. Here's what I'm doing about it." That's not positive or negative. It's steady. And steady is what people need when the ground is shifting. Not certainty — nobody has certainty during a reorg. Just the knowledge that someone is paying attention, making decisions, and telling them the truth as it becomes available.

Not every reorg arrives as an earthquake. Sometimes it's a slow tide — things shifting gradually until the landscape is unrecognizable. That's what Vikram Desai was navigating.

Let me tell you about Vikram Desai.

Vikram was a VP of engineering at a mid-size technology company that had done a round of layoffs six months before we started working together. The company had let go of one of its most beloved leaders — someone the rank and file considered a cornerstone. The official explanation was "org design," but nobody bought it. If this person could be let go, the thinking went, nobody was safe.

Vikram had stepped up immediately. He did what strong leaders do in crisis: he did damage control, he smoothed things over, he had individual conversations with the people who were most shaken. And then he did something smart. He gave a presentation that clarified roles and responsibilities for all of engineering and product from that point on.

"It's amazing how far it goes when people are feeling scared and uncertain and they just know: here's what I'm working on, here's my role within that, here's who I go to," he told me. "That's all they wanted. Clarity."

But here was Vikram's own struggle: while he was stabilizing everyone else, he was also trying to figure out his own strategic positioning in the new structure. He had an opportunity to seize – the reorg had created a leadership vacuum in a critical area, and he was one of two or three people who could fill it. But he was nervous about being too aggressive. He didn't want to come across as "trying to take turf away from others."

> ***"Never let a good reorg go to waste."***

That sounds cynical. It's not. What I mean is this: disruption creates opportunity. The same chaos that makes everyone anxious also creates openings that didn't exist before. New roles. New reporting structures. New needs. The leaders who thrive in change aren't the ones who duck and cover. They're the ones who stabilize their teams and position themselves for what comes next. Those aren't contradictory. They're complementary.

Vikram was wrestling with this tension: wanting to be a good citizen who focused on his people versus wanting to seize an opportunity that might not come again. I told him those weren't in conflict. "The best thing you can do for your team is to be in a strong position. If you grow, they grow. If you get the bigger scope, your people get more exposure, more opportunity, more resources. Advocating for yourself and stabilizing your team are the same thing when you do them together."

He made his move. He put together a brief proposal for how the leadership vacuum could be filled, positioned it as a solution to an organizational problem rather than a personal ask, and presented it to his boss. He got the expanded scope. And the way he got it — with clarity, with a focus on organizational need, with his team's stability as the foundation — actually strengthened his credibility with the leadership team.

Compare that with Nathan's peer who was grabbing turf under the cover of chaos. She got territory. But she also got a reputation. And reputations outlast reorgs.

> ***Change doesn't close all the doors. It rearranges them. Your job is to notice which new ones are opening.***

## THE REFRAME

The professionals who thrive in change aren't the ones who avoid chaos. They're the ones who've built systems for operating within it.

A reorg is a forced altitude reset. Everyone's position just shifted, and the leaders who recalibrate fastest — who figure out what "at my altitude" means in the new structure — are the ones who come out stronger.

I worked with a leader whose company was merging with a UK-based firm. She was treating the merger entirely as a threat — more uncertainty, more politics, more risk to her role. I asked her, "What could the consolidation bring in terms of more receptivity to what you're doing? The UK firm has a completely different structure around the kind of work you lead. What if they actually value this function more than your current firm does?"

She hadn't considered that. Because when we're in threat mode, we only see doors closing. We don't notice the new ones that might be opening.

Nathan's reframe was different. His natural strength was leading through chaos. He'd done it his entire career. The question wasn't whether he could handle it — he clearly could. The question was whether he was going to burn himself out handling it for everyone else while ignoring what it was doing to him.

Because here's what I see with leaders during change: they pour everything into stabilizing their team and their organization, and they treat their own wellbeing as an afterthought. That works for a week. It doesn't work for six months. The leaders who survive sustained change are the ones who manage their own energy as deliberately as they manage their team's morale.

There's one more thing about change that nobody says out loud: sometimes the reorg reveals something you've been avoiding. Sometimes the new structure makes it undeniably clear that the organization doesn't value what you do, or that the culture has shifted away from what you need, or that the person you're now reporting to is someone you fundamentally can't work with.

That's not a reorg problem. That's a clarity gift. The disruption stripped away the ambiguity you were hiding behind. And now you have a real decision to make — one that was always there, but that the old structure let you avoid.

Some people hear that and get scared. I think it should be liberating. Because the worst place to be in your career isn't in a bad situation. It's in a bad situation that you can't see clearly. The reorg just turned the lights on. What you do with that visibility is up to you.

## THE FRAMEWORK

You can't control a reorg. I learned that the hard way — more than once. What you can control is how you lead through it. These tools help you sort what's yours to manage from what isn't, communicate when you don't have answers, and take care of the people who are looking to you for stability they can't find anywhere else.

***Tool #1: The Three Circles of Control.*** I started using this framework with my own teams during a particularly brutal reorg early in my career — the kind where you're reassuring people during the day and updating your own resume at night. What I discovered is that the fastest way to regain focus is to separate your world into three circles. What you can control — your communication, your team's priorities, your own preparation, your relationships. What you can influence — how decisions are framed, who has access to information, how your work is positioned. What you can't affect — the board's decision, the market conditions, the CEO's strategy, the partner vote.

**THE THREE CIRCLES**

*"Where is your energy actually going?"*

Spend 90 percent of your energy in circles one and two. Circle three is where anxiety lives. Most professionals spend far too much time there because it feels important. It is important. But worrying about it doesn't change it. The leaders who stay effective during disruption are the ones who can acknowledge the things they can't control without letting those things consume their energy.

***Tool #2: The Over-Communication Principle.*** During uncertainty, communicate three times more than you think is necessary. People don't hear you the first time. They're processing their own anxiety while you're talking. By the third time, it starts to land.

It's not just the message — it's the consistency. When people see you saying the same things repeatedly, it signals stability.

But over-communication isn't just broadcasting — it's also listening. One of the most common mistakes I see during organizational change is leaders who communicate constantly but only in one direction. They send updates, hold town halls, craft talking points — and never create a space for people to ask questions, push back, or say what they're actually feeling. Communication during change has to be a conversation, not a memo. Ask your team what they're hearing. Ask what they're worried about. And then respond — even if the response is "I don't know yet, but I hear you." That response alone does more for trust than any perfectly crafted announcement.

***Tool #3: The Retention Conversation.*** This is situational – you won't need it every week. But when you do, five minutes can save you your best person. If you're a leader with key people you can't afford to lose, don't rely on loyalty or culture to keep them. Have direct conversations. The biggest mistake I see leaders make during disruption is withholding information because they think silence protects people. It doesn't. It sends them to LinkedIn.

Be honest about what you know and what you don't. "Here's what I can tell you. Here's what I don't know yet. Here's when I expect to know more. And here's what I want you to know: you matter to this team and I'm fighting for this group." That conversation takes five minutes. And it's the difference between someone staying and someone quietly accepting a recruiter's call.

I worked with a leader who learned this the hard way. After a reorg, he assumed his best people knew they were valued because he'd always treated them well. He didn't have the explicit conversation. Three weeks later, his strongest senior engineer accepted an offer at a competitor. When he asked why, the engineer said, "I didn't know where I stood in the new structure and nobody told me."

"Nobody told me." Not "I wasn't valued." Not "I was treated badly." Just "nobody told me." The silence was the problem. And it was entirely preventable with a five-minute conversation.

***Tool #4: The Opportunity Scan.*** This is not about opportunism. It's about awareness — and the window for it is narrow. While you're stabilizing, keep one eye on what's opening up. New roles. New reporting structures. Projects that need leadership. Relationships that are suddenly accessible because the old hierarchy dissolved. Don't feel guilty about this — it's not opportunism. It's awareness. And the leaders who emerge from change in stronger positions are always the ones who were paying attention while everyone else was only reacting.

I want to be specific about what opportunity scanning looks like because I've seen people do it well and I've seen people do it badly. Doing it well means quietly building relationships with the new stakeholders, understanding the new priorities, and positioning your team's work in terms of what the organization needs next — not what it needed before. Doing it badly means transparently grabbing for territory while your peers are still processing the shock. The former builds your reputation. The latter damages it in ways that outlast the reorg.

Timing matters. The first two weeks belong to stabilization — take care of your people, communicate relentlessly. After that, start scanning. The initial shock has worn off and the organization is figuring out its new shape.

One of my clients described this perfectly: "Week one, I was a firefighter. Week three, I was an architect." That's the transition. You can't be the architect while the building is still on fire. But once the fire is out, someone has to design what comes next. Make sure you're in the room for that conversation.

## THE EXPERIMENT

If you're currently in a period of organizational change, write down everything that's occupying your mental energy. Put each item into one of the three circles. For anything in the "can't affect" circle, consciously choose to release it for one week. See what happens to your energy and your focus.

Then look at your communication: Have you told your team everything they need to know? Have you told them the same thing at least three times? Have you had individual conversations with the people you most need to keep? If you haven't done all three, start there. Today.

And if you're not currently in change — bookmark this chapter. You will be.

## THE MIRROR

These questions apply whether you're mid-reorg or in a period of relative calm. Because preparation for change happens before the change, not during it.

- How much of your current stress is about things you can actually affect versus things that are out of your control? Be honest about the ratio.

- What new doors might be opening that you haven't noticed because you're focused on the ones closing?

- Are you over-communicating with your team during this change, or are you assuming they know more than they do? When's the last time you said the same important message three times?

- Who are the key people you can't afford to lose? Do they know that? Have you given them a reason to stay beyond inertia?

- Is this the kind of change that requires you to adapt, or is this the signal that it's time to move on? How would you know the difference?

- When the dust settles, what position do you want to be in? Are you doing anything today to move toward that position, or are you just surviving?

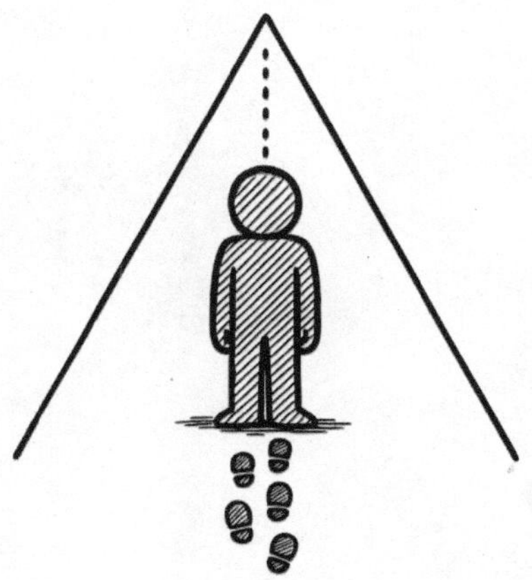

## PART 4

# THE LONG GAME

*Building a Career That Doesn't Cost You Everything Else*

---

*At some point, the conversation shifts from "How do I succeed in this role?" to "What am I building, and is it actually what I want?" The chapters in this section are about the questions that take years to ask and minutes to answer once you stop avoiding them.*

## CHAPTER TEN

# WHEN TO STAY AND WHEN TO GO

*How to make career decisions from clarity instead of fear*

---

*"I'm not unhappy exactly. I'm just not sure this is where I should be anymore."*

**— A VP who had been in the same role for five years**

## THE PATTERN

This is the conversation nobody prepares you for. And it's a different kind of altitude problem — not about how you operate in the role, but about whether you should still be in it. Not the performance review conversation, not the difficult feedback conversation, not even the reorg conversation. The one where you sit across from yourself and ask: Should I still be here?

It comes in different packages. Sometimes it's the executive who has been promoted three times at the same company and is starting to feel like the walls are closing in. Sometimes it's the person who just survived a reorg and is wondering whether the company that emerges is one they want to work for. Sometimes it's the leader who is performing well by every metric but hasn't felt energized by the work in two years.

Let me tell you about Rachel Novak.

Rachel was a VP of operations at a consumer technology company. She'd been there for seven years. She'd built her team from the ground up. She had vesting equity, a boss she respected, and a brand on her resume that opened doors.

And she was quietly suffocating.

Not from overwork. Not from a bad manager. From something harder to articulate: the sense that she had outgrown the role but hadn't outgrown the comfort. The work was familiar. The routines were established. The paycheck was generous. And the equity vesting schedule was designed — quite deliberately — to make leaving feel financially irrational.

Rachel called it "golden handcuffs," which is what everyone calls it. But when I pushed her on it, the handcuffs weren't really golden. They were a story she was telling herself about risk. The equity was meaningful but not life-changing. The salary could be matched elsewhere. What was actually keeping her wasn't the money. It was the fear of starting over. Of being the new person. Of losing the institutional knowledge and relationships she'd spent seven years building.

I hear some version of this every month. "I can't leave because of the equity." "I can't leave because of the relationships." And when I push on each one, it usually collapses. The equity math rarely works out when you run the numbers. The relationships are more portable than you think. And the "proving yourself" part is real, but it's a temporary cost, not a permanent condition.

What's really keeping most people stuck isn't the tangible stuff. It's the story they've built around the tangible stuff. The story that says leaving is irresponsible, risky, ungrateful. The story that says comfort is the same as success. The story that says staying is a choice when it's really just the absence of a different choice.

She was in survival mode. Not surviving a crisis — surviving comfort. And survival mode, regardless of what you're surviving, makes you small. It narrows your field of vision. It makes you optimize for keeping what you have instead of pursuing what you want.

I see this pattern often. Leaders who are objectively successful but privately stagnant. They've achieved a level of professional comfort that is simultaneously their greatest asset and their biggest liability. The comfort funds their lifestyle. But it also funds their inertia. And the longer they stay in that zone, the harder it becomes to leave — not because the opportunities get worse, but because the fear of disrupting what works gets stronger.

Rachel's breakthrough came when I asked her to separate the role from the environment. She loved the kind of work she did. She'd lost the energy for the specific context she was doing it in. Those are very different diagnoses with very different solutions. One says "change careers." The other says "change settings." When she realized the issue was the setting — not the work itself — the decision became much clearer. She didn't need to reinvent herself. She needed to transplant herself.

Six months later she left. She took a comparable role at a smaller, faster-growing company. Less equity. More energy. She told me in our final session, "I should have done this two years ago. The only thing the golden handcuffs were attached to was my fear."

> ***The most dangerous career trap isn't a bad job. It's a good-enough job that slowly becomes the ceiling you didn't choose.***

Now let me give you the other side, because this chapter isn't about encouraging everyone to quit their job. It's about making the decision from clarity instead of emotion.

Let me tell you about Derek Huang.

Derek was a director of engineering at a SaaS company going through a rough patch — revenue down, two rounds of layoffs, morale low. He was doing good work, but the environment was grinding him down, and recruiters were calling weekly with offers that looked shinier than what he had.

Derek wanted to leave. The pull was strong. But when we unpacked it, his desire to leave was almost entirely reactive. He wasn't running toward something. He was running away from discomfort. And the things making him uncomfortable — the organizational uncertainty, the pressure, the ambiguity — were things he'd face at any company going through growth or change.

> ***"Shopping doesn't mean buying."***

I had a client who did what he called his "spring fling" — every spring for almost 25 years, he'd go out and interview. Not because he wanted to leave. Because he wanted to choose to stay. He'd take recruiter calls, meet with hiring managers, go through a few rounds. And then he'd either find something actually better — which happened twice in 25 years — or he'd come back to his current role with fresh perspective on what he had.

That practice is brilliant for several reasons. It keeps your interview skills current. It gives you real market data about your value. It prevents the golden-handcuffs narrative from taking root because you're regularly testing whether the grass is actually greener. And it transforms staying from a passive default into an active choice. There's a profound psychological difference between "I'm still here because I haven't left" and "I'm still here because I looked at the alternatives and chose this."

Derek didn't leave. He took a few calls, explored two opportunities seriously, and realized that the problems he was running from weren't specific to his company. They were specific to his level. And changing companies wouldn't change his level. It would just reset his relationships and institutional knowledge back to zero.

That's a critical distinction. Some problems are environmental — they're about this company, this boss, this culture. Those problems are solved by leaving. But some problems are altitude problems — they're about the challenges inherent to your level of seniority, and they'll follow you wherever you go. Organizational politics exists at every company. Ambiguity exists in every leadership role. Difficult peers are universal. If the problem is the altitude, changing the mountain doesn't help.

Derek recognized this and made a different decision. Instead of leaving, he invested in changing how he operated within his current environment. He started managing up more effectively. He built stronger relationships with the peers who had influence. He redefined the boundaries of his role to include more of the strategic work that energized him. Within six months, the job he'd wanted to leave felt like a different job. Same company. Same title. Different experience. Because he'd changed the variable that actually mattered: himself.

## THE REFRAME

Here's the framework I use for stay-or-go decisions. There are really only three valid reasons to leave a role:

One: You've stopped growing. Not "this quarter is boring" — you've hit the ceiling of what this role, this team, and this organization can teach you. You've been saying "I'll grow next quarter" for four quarters in a row, and nothing has changed. That's a signal.

Two: The environment is fundamentally broken. Not "my boss is annoying" — the culture, values, or leadership are misaligned with who you are in ways that won't change. You've tried to influence it, you've tried to adapt, and the gap remains. At some point, adaptation becomes self-erasure.

Three: A meaningfully better opportunity exists. Not "a recruiter said exciting things" — you've done the homework. You understand the role, the team, the culture, the trajectory. And it's meaningfully better in ways that matter to you, not just different.

Everything else is noise. Frustration with a project. A bad quarter. A difficult peer. Compensation envy. Those are problems to solve, not reasons to leave. And the professionals who build the strongest long-term careers are the ones who can distinguish between "I need to leave" and "I need to change something about how I'm operating here."

I'll share one more lens that helps people with this decision. I call it the Sunday Night Test. When Sunday evening comes around and you think about Monday morning, what do you feel? If it's neutral or mildly positive — the normal resistance anyone feels about ending a weekend — you're probably fine. If it's dread — a weight in your chest, an anxiety that doesn't go away, a feeling of being trapped — that's data. And if it's been dread for more than three months straight, that's a pattern, not a phase.

THE RENTAL MINDSET

*You moved in. But you never unpacked.*

I use another analogy that clients find helpful: think of your relationship with your job like owning a house, renting an apartment, or staying in a hotel. When you own the house, you invest in it — you renovate, you maintain, you build for the long term. When you're renting, you keep it nice but you're not knocking down walls. When you're in a hotel, you're just passing through.

Most people should be treating their current role like they own the house. But if you've decided — decided — actually decided, not just fantasized — that you're leaving, then shift to renting. Stop investing in the long-term renovations. Focus on what matters for the transition. Just be honest with yourself about which mode you're in. The worst place to be is renting while pretending you own — or owning while secretly wanting to leave.

I've seen both. The leader who tells everyone she's committed while quietly interviewing on Tuesdays — that's renting while pretending to own. Her team can feel the half-heartedness even if they can't name it. And the leader who keeps volunteering for three-year initiatives while knowing in his gut that he needs to move on — that's owning while wanting to leave. He's making commitments his heart isn't in, and eventually both he and the organization will pay for that misalignment.

Ask yourself right now: am I an owner, a renter, or a hotel guest in this role? There's no wrong answer. But there's a wrong answer you're not admitting to.

One more thing about the spring fling practice, because I think it's the single most underused career tool I know. The leader who taught me this had been doing it for 25 years. Every spring. He'd update his resume, take two or three recruiter calls, and go through at least one full interview process. Most years, nothing came of it. Twice, it led to a move that transformed his career.

> ***"What if" is a career killer. Not because the answer is always 'leave.' Usually it's 'stay.' But the uncertainty of not knowing is corrosive.***

## THE FRAMEWORK

I've watched a lot of career decisions over 30 years — my own and my clients'. The ones made from fear or frustration tend to look good for about six months. The ones made from clarity tend to hold. These tools help you figure out which kind of decision you're about to make.

***Tool #1: The Energy Audit.*** For two weeks, track your energy at the end of each workday. Not your productivity — your energy. On a scale of 1 to 10, how depleted or energized do you feel? At the end of two weeks, look at the pattern. If you're consistently below a five, that's data. If certain activities or people correlate with the lows, that's data you can use. Sometimes the audit reveals that you don't need a new job — you need to restructure the one you have.

I had a client who was convinced she needed to leave her company. The energy audit told a different story. Her energy was high on Mondays and Tuesdays when she was doing strategic work with her team. It cratered on Wednesdays and Thursdays when she was in back-to-back cross-functional meetings that she didn't need to attend. By Friday she was so depleted she couldn't think straight. The problem wasn't the company. It was her Wednesday and Thursday schedule. She eliminated four meetings, delegated two others, and her energy came back to a level she hadn't felt in a year. Same company. Same role. Completely different experience.

The energy audit works because it gives you data instead of feelings. "I'm unhappy at work" is a feeling. "My energy drops below a three every Wednesday after the cross-functional sync" is data. And data can be acted on.

***Tool #2: The Spring Fling.*** This is a once-a-year practice, not a daily one. But the leaders who do it consistently make better career decisions than those who don't. Once a year, take a few recruiter calls. Go through at least one interview process. Not to leave — to calibrate. What's your market value? What are other companies offering? What excites you? What doesn't? This practice removes the desperation from job searching because you're doing it from a position of strength, not crisis. And it ensures that staying is always a choice, never a default.

***Tool #3: The Two-Year Test.*** Ask yourself: If nothing changes about this role in the next two years, am I okay with that? Not "will I survive" — am I actually okay with it? If the answer is no, then you need to either change something real about the role or start building your exit. Two years is long enough to be honest and short enough to force a real answer.

***Tool #4: The Non-Negotiables List.*** Write down your five non-negotiable requirements for a role. Not nice-to-haves. Non-negotiables. Things you will not compromise on. Then assess your current role against that list. If it meets four out of five, you're probably in a good place. If it meets two out of five, that's a problem. And the clarity of the list itself is valuable — most people have never actually articulated what they need. They just have a vague sense of dissatisfaction without a framework for diagnosing it.

## THE EXPERIMENT

Write down three things: Why did you take this job? Why are you still here? And what would need to change for you to leave?

If the answer to the first question is very different from the answer to the second question, pay attention to that gap. It might mean you've grown past your original reasons. It might mean the role has changed. Or it might mean you've been on autopilot for longer than you realized.

Then try the spring fling. Take one recruiter call this month. Not to leave. To choose.

Pay attention to how you feel after the call. If you feel relieved to come back to what you have — that's data. If you feel a pull toward something you heard — that's also data. And if you feel nothing at all, that numbness is the most important data point of the three. It usually means you've been on autopilot so long that your ability to evaluate has atrophied. That's worth sitting with before you make any decision in either direction.

## THE MIRROR

These are the questions most people avoid for years. Don't.

- Are you staying because you're choosing this, or because leaving feels too risky? What would change if you separated the decision from the fear?
- When's the last time you felt actually excited about your work — not satisfied, not comfortable, but excited? How long ago was that?

- What are your golden handcuffs made of? Are they actually golden, or are they stories about risk that you haven't tested?
- If you could design your ideal role from scratch, how much of it overlaps with what you're doing now? What's missing?
- Are you growing, or are you repeating? Be honest. Mastery feels like growth but it isn't always.
- What would you tell a friend in your exact situation? The advice you'd give them is probably the advice you need to hear.

CHAPTER ELEVEN

# THE BURNOUT YOU DON'T SEE COMING

*Why the most dangerous kind of exhaustion is the kind you've normalized*

---

*"I'm not burned out. I'm just... always tired."*

**— A director who hadn't taken a real vacation in two years**

## THE PATTERN

Burnout doesn't announce itself. It doesn't walk in the door with a sign. It accumulates. And here's what connects it to everything we've covered so far: every altitude problem in this book — the wrong work, the imposter, the avoided conversation, the political blindness — burns energy. Burnout is what happens when you've been spending that energy for too long without replenishing it. It's the extra hour on Tuesday that becomes the extra hour every day. It's the working vacation that becomes every vacation. It's the Sunday-night anxiety that was once occasional and is now the norm.

I've worked with an alarming number of professionals who got to burnout, and I can tell you this: not a single one of them realized they were burned out until they already were. Every one of them thought they were managing it. Every one of them had a story about why their pace was necessary. And every one of them was wrong.

Let me tell you about Karen Ellsworth.

Karen was a senior director at a healthcare company. She ran a team of 35 people across three time zones. She was the kind of leader everyone relied on — her team, her peers, her boss. She picked up the phone at nine on a Friday night. She said yes to every cross-functional request. She worked 60-hour weeks and told herself it was temporary.

It wasn't temporary. It had been three years.

Karen's burnout didn't look like exhaustion. It looked like efficiency. She had optimized every minute of her day. She was productive, organized, responsive. From the outside, she was thriving. From the inside, she was running on fumes and hadn't felt genuine enthusiasm about her work in over a year.

When I asked her what a sustainable work week looked like, she paused for a long time. "I don't know," she said. "I don't know what that would look like for me."

That answer – "I don't know" – is the most reliable indicator of burnout I've found. Not anger, not frustration, not fatigue. The inability to even imagine what a healthy pace would feel like. When you've been running so long that you've forgotten what walking feels like, you're burned out. Even if you don't feel burned out. Especially if you don't feel burned out.

Here's what had happened to Karen: she'd started her career working 50 hours because the company needed it. Then she got promoted and worked 55 because the scope demanded it. Then she built a team and worked 60 because she couldn't let go of the work she'd been doing before the promotion. Each increment was small. Each one was justified. And the cumulative effect was that she'd normalized a pace that would have horrified her 10 years earlier.

I asked her, "When's the last time you took a real vacation? Not a working vacation – a real one. No email. No Slack. Phone in a drawer."

She thought about it. "Two years ago. And I checked email every morning before the kids woke up."

"So the answer is never," I said.

That landed hard. But it needed to. Because Karen wasn't going to change anything until she stopped telling herself the story that her pace was temporary. It wasn't temporary. It was her life. And she was the only person who could change it.

> ***Burnout doesn't feel like collapse. It just feels normal. That's why you don't see it coming.***

I want to talk about the mechanism here because understanding how burnout builds is the only way to prevent it.

Let me tell you about Francesca Diaz.

Francesca was a director of program management at a retail company. She described herself as "an automatic yes machine." Every request that came in, she said yes. Not because she was a pushover – because she wanted to help. She had an abundance of good intention that was slowly destroying her.

I told her, "Automatic yes machines have one eventual outcome. What do you think that is?"

She laughed. "Burnout."

"It's a one-way train," I said. "There's no other destination. And what happens with an overloaded backlog? Every item in that backlog is telling you something. It's saying: you have more work than you can do well, you're going to start cutting corners, quality is going to drop, and eventually you're going to resent the work you used to love."

But here was the harder part of the conversation: Francesca hadn't just created this pattern. She'd trained the people around her to expect it. She'd established a reputation as the person who always said yes, always delivered, always found a way. And now, any time she pushed back, people ignored the pushback – because they knew from years of experience that she'd do it anyway.

"We've trained our customers to treat us this way," I told her. "No villains here. But if we want them to treat us differently, we have to retrain them. And retraining is harder than training because we're fighting against years of precedent."

That retraining started with one word: no. Not an aggressive no. Not a dramatic no. Just a calm, clear, "I can't take that on right now. Here's what I can do." The first few times she said it, people were surprised. Some pushed harder. But within a month, the dynamic started to shift. People brought her fewer low-priority requests. They started solving things themselves that they would have previously dropped on her desk. And Francesca's backlog — for the first time in years — started to shrink.

Burnout is almost never caused by one thing. It's caused by a system of behaviors and habits you've built — often with the best intentions — that is now consuming you.

## THE REFRAME

I told one of my clients something that changed how he thought about time: "Every minute over 40 hours that you work is borrowed from somewhere. Where are you borrowing it from?"

He didn't have an answer at first. So I helped him find it. "You're borrowing it from sleep, from your family, from exercise, from the things that actually recharge you so that you can be effective during those 40 hours. And the interest rate on that loan is brutal. Because unlike financial debt, energy debt compounds invisibly. You don't see the bill until your body or your relationships present it to you."

He had a habit of checking his resting heart rate every morning. I told him to start treating it as a burnout metric. When it trends up over weeks, that's stress accumulating. When it doesn't come down on weekends, that's recovery failing. Your body keeps a better scorecard than your mind does. Your mind will tell you you're fine. Your body won't lie.

Here's the reframe I offer to everyone on this topic: the organization benefits from your burnout. Not intentionally — but a burned-out high performer who says yes to everything is the best deal the company ever got. They get 60-hour weeks at the price of 40, and they never have to address the structural problem because you keep absorbing it. Sustainability isn't a luxury. It's the moment you stop subsidizing a broken system with your own health. The leaders who are still sharp, still energized, still producing their best work 10 years into their career are not the ones who sprinted the hardest. They're the ones who paced themselves. They built recovery into their rhythm instead of treating it as something to earn after the crisis passed.

The crisis never passes. There's always another one. If you're waiting for things to calm down before you take care of yourself, you'll be waiting forever.

One of my clients went on a vacation and when she came back, her VP told her boss that she "doesn't care about the success of the project" because she'd been unreachable. This same person had just received a high-performer rating. The message was clear: your performance doesn't matter if your presence doesn't match expectations, even during time off. And that's the culture most professionals are operating in. A culture that rewards availability over sustainability and then acts surprised when people burn out.

You have to push back on that culture. Not with a manifesto. With boundaries that you enforce consistently, quietly, and without apology.

Let me tell you what that actually looks like in practice, because "set boundaries" is easy advice that's hard to execute.

I worked with a leader who was great at setting boundaries in her personal life but terrible at it professionally. When I pointed out the contradiction, she laughed. "At home, if someone crosses a line, I have no problem saying so. At work, I just... absorb it."

The reason was simple: at home, she didn't fear consequences for holding a boundary. At work, she feared being seen as uncommitted, not a team player, not willing to go the extra mile. And so she absorbed and absorbed and absorbed until there was nothing left to absorb.

I told her, "You already know how to do this. You do it every day at home. The only thing that's different at work is the story you're telling yourself about what holding a boundary means. At home, it means self-respect. At work, you've convinced yourself it means selfishness. It's the same skill. You just need to apply it in a different context."

She started small. She stopped answering Slack messages after eight p.m. She blocked 90 minutes every morning for focused work and declined meetings that conflicted with it. She told her team, "Unless it's a genuine emergency, it can wait until morning."

The first week was hard. She kept reaching for her phone. The second week was easier. By the third week, her team had adjusted. They solved more things on their own. The things that seemed urgent at nine p.m. turned out to be perfectly manageable at nine a.m. And the world — as it always does when leaders set boundaries — kept turning.

The deeper insight here is that boundaries don't just protect you. They develop your team. When you're always available, your team never has to figure things out on their own. When you create space, they fill it with capability. Your burnout and your team's underdevelopment are often the same problem with the same solution. And there's a layer underneath that: when you model unsustainable behavior, you're teaching your team that this is what leadership looks like. You're not just burning yourself out — you're building a culture that burns out the next generation of leaders behind you.

> ***Every minute over 40 hours is borrowed from somewhere. And the interest rate on energy debt is brutal.***

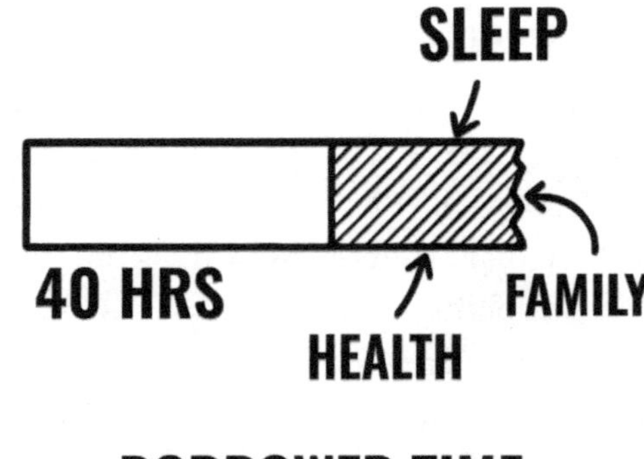


**BORROWED TIME**

*Every hour over 40 is borrowed-from sleep, from family, from health.*

## THE FRAMEWORK

Burnout doesn't announce itself. It normalizes. And by the time most people notice it, they've been running on fumes for months. These tools help you see what you've stopped seeing — the patterns you've built, the energy you're spending, and the recovery you've stopped protecting.

***Tool #1: The Monster Audit.*** I told a client who was drowning in her team's dependency on her: "You've created a little bit of a monster. That's okay — we all do it. But now's the time to tame the monster and start shrinking it." Do your own monster audit. What patterns have you created that are now consuming you? What did you set up out of good intention that has become unsustainable? Name the monsters. That's the first step to shrinking them.

Let me give you some common monsters I see, because naming them makes them easier to recognize. The "I'll just do it myself" monster: you took on a task temporarily and it became permanent because you never handed it back. The "always available" monster: you answered one late-night message and now your team expects you to be on call 24 hours a day. The "only I can do this" monster: you've convinced yourself that a particular process requires your personal touch, when the real reason you haven't delegated it is that you enjoy the control. The "automatic yes" monster: you said yes to one cross-functional request and now every team in the company thinks you're the person who never says no.

Each of these started with a good intention. Each one became a monster we let out of its cage. Pick one — the one costing you the most energy — and shrink it by 10 percent this month. Then another 10 percent next month. By the end of the quarter, it's half the size it was.

**THE MONSTER**

*It grows every day you don't name it.*

***Tool #2: The Five-Hour Experiment.*** If you're working 50 or more hours a week, give yourself a goal: cut five hours over the next two weeks. Not by working faster. By eliminating or delegating five hours of work that either doesn't need to be done or doesn't need to be done by you. This is harder than it sounds because you'll immediately generate reasons why every hour is essential. Challenge those reasons. Most of them are habits, not necessities.

***Tool #3: The Non-Negotiable Recovery.*** Pick one thing that recharges you — exercise, time with family, a hobby, sleep — and make it non-negotiable. Not "I'll try to do it." Non-negotiable. Like brushing your teeth. I make my own non-negotiables on a daily schedule: specific tasks on specific days, so nothing stacks up. There are days I wake up and I don't want to do what's on the list. I don't give myself the option to skip it. I just get it done, and then it's done, and the reward is I don't have to think about it again.

That discipline sounds rigid. It's actually the opposite. It's freedom. Because the things that recharge you can't compete with the things that deplete you if they're optional. They have to be protected.

***Tool #4: The Body Scorecard.*** This is the most objective tool in the book — no self-deception possible when you're looking at data. Track one physical metric for two weeks — resting heart rate, sleep quality, or how many days you wake up already tired. When your resting heart rate trends up over weeks, that's stress accumulating. When it doesn't come down on weekends, that's recovery failing. I had a client who insisted he wasn't burned out until he looked at his fitness tracker data. His resting heart rate had climbed eight beats per minute over three months. His sleep efficiency had dropped from 85% to 72%. His body had been keeping score the whole time — he just hadn't been reading the scorecard. The data gave him something his feelings couldn't: objectivity. It's hard to argue with a graph that shows your body is running hotter every week.

**On the stay-or-go question:** If the audit reveals that the role itself — not the hours or the habits — is the primary source of exhaustion, the house/renter/hotel distinction in Chapter 10 applies here. The question of whether to adapt or leave is a separate decision from the question of how to recover. Treat them separately.

## THE EXPERIMENT

This week, track every hour you work. Not a rough estimate — actual hours. At the end of the week, look at the number. Then ask yourself: Where did those extra hours come from? What didn't happen because of them?

Then identify your three biggest monsters — the three patterns you've created that are consuming the most energy. For each one, write down one specific action you could take to start shrinking it. Not eliminating it overnight. Just shrinking it. A monster that's five percent smaller this month is 50 percent smaller by the end of the year.

And take your vacation. Your actual vacation. Not the kind where you check email by the pool. The kind where you're unreachable. If the thought of being unreachable for a week makes you anxious, that's your answer. That anxiety is the burnout talking. The work will survive without you. It always does.

## THE MIRROR

- How many hours did you work last week? Now ask your partner or your closest friend how many they think you worked. What does the gap between those numbers tell you?

- What would a sustainable pace actually look like for you? Can you describe it in concrete terms — specific hours, specific boundaries, specific routines? If you can't, that's the problem.

- What have you trained the people around you to expect from you? Is that expectation sustainable? If not, what's the first boundary you need to set?

- When's the last time you took a real vacation — fully disconnected, no email, no Slack? What does your answer tell you?

- What's the monster you've created that's consuming the most energy? What would it take to shrink it by 10 percent?

- If you burned out tomorrow and had to take a month off, what would happen to your team? If the answer is "they'd be fine," then your current pace isn't necessary. If the answer is "it would collapse," then your current pace isn't sustainable. Either way, something needs to change.

# CHAPTER TWELVE

# DEFINING YOUR OWN GOOD ENOUGH

*How to build a career and a life on your own terms*

---

*"I keep chasing the next thing. And I'm starting to wonder what I'm actually chasing."*

**— A senior leader, in our final session**

# THE PATTERN

This is the chapter I almost didn't write. Not because it's the hardest to articulate – although it is – but because every other chapter in this book helps you perform better at altitude. This one asks whether you're at the right altitude in the first place – and the message runs directly counter to everything our professional culture teaches us. We are taught to want more. More scope, more title, more compensation, more impact. The entire machinery of career development is designed to keep you climbing.

And at some point, some of you will need to stop climbing and start asking: What am I climbing toward?

Let me tell you about Marcus Keane. Marcus was a General Manager at a hospitality and entertainment company – the kind of executive role that sounds impressive at dinner parties and grinds you to dust in between them. He was responsible for multiple locations, 100s of employees, revenue targets that moved every quarter, and a schedule that had consumed his evenings and most of his weekends for the better part of a decade.

He came to coaching not because he was struggling – but because he'd achieved everything he'd set out to achieve and felt nothing. Not unhappy. Not burned out. Just... empty. The wins didn't land anymore. The promotions were nice but not satisfying. He'd reached the altitude he'd been climbing toward and discovered that the view wasn't what he expected.

I asked him the question I ask everyone who arrives at this place: "What does good look like for you? Not for the company. Not for your boss. Not for your resume. For you. In the three areas that matter – work, family, and self."

He couldn't answer it.

Not because he was inarticulate. Because he'd never been asked. In 20 years of performance reviews, development plans, and leadership programs, no one had ever asked Marcus to define what good looked like on his own terms. The definitions had always been provided for him. Good meant higher. Good meant more. Good meant the next rung.

He'd been climbing someone else's ladder his entire career. And he was only now realizing it.

Marcus was functional, effective, and respected. The people around him had no idea anything was wrong. That's the insidious part: when you're successful by every external measure, nobody checks on you. The emptiness is invisible to everyone except you.

I asked Marcus to do something radical by corporate standards: stop. Just stop for a moment and articulate what he actually wanted. Not what the next logical career step was. Not what the compensation committee would approve. What he wanted. For his mornings. For his weekends. For the next decade of his life.

It took him three sessions to get there. Not because the answers were complicated. Because he'd spent so long suppressing the question that the muscle for answering it had atrophied. He'd become so good at optimizing for organizational outcomes that he'd lost the ability to optimize for personal ones.

When he finally articulated it, it was surprisingly simple. He wanted to do meaningful work. He wanted to be home for dinner more often than not. He wanted a hobby that had nothing to do with leadership. And he wanted to stop feeling like every Sunday night was the beginning of an endurance test.

None of those things required him to quit his job or take a pay cut or become a different person. They required him to define "good" on his own terms and then make decisions accordingly. Which, it turns out, is the hardest thing of all.

> ***At some point, you have to stop asking "What's next?" and start asking "What's enough?"***

Marcus was at the top. But this question doesn't need to wait until you get there.

Let me tell you about Joanna Park.

Joanna was a senior director at a technology company. She was in her early forties, two young kids, a partner who also worked demanding hours. She was performing well, getting promoted on a regular cadence, and doing all the things that are supposed to signal a thriving career.

But she came to coaching with a question that surprised me in its directness: "How do I chase my north star while also being a present parent? Because right now I feel like I'm failing at both."

Joanna was a self-described "North Star, Polaris kind of person." She liked having direction. She liked having a target. But she had three targets that were all competing for the same finite resource: her time and energy. Work wanted more of her. Her family needed more of her. And she — the actual person underneath the VP title and the parent role — had disappeared entirely.

I asked her to do something that sounds simple but turned out to be one of the hardest exercises she'd done: identify three to five non-negotiables in each of the three areas – work, family, and self. Not goals. Not aspirations. Non-negotiables. The things that, if they aren't happening, nothing else matters.

For work, her non-negotiables included being in a role where she was learning and having at least one project that felt actually strategic. For family, it was being present for bedtime at least four nights a week and one full weekend day with no work. For self – and this was the hardest list – it was exercise three times a week and one hour per week of something that had nothing to do with work or parenting.

When she looked at her actual calendar, she was meeting her work non-negotiables. She was meeting most of her family non-negotiables. And she was meeting zero of her self non-negotiables. Zero.

"That's where the failing-at-everything feeling is coming from," I told her. "You're not failing at everything. You're failing at yourself. And when we neglect ourselves, everything else starts to feel inadequate because we're running on empty."

Joanna's response was one I've heard from dozens of high-performing professionals: "But when am I supposed to do those things? There literally aren't enough hours."

And she was right – if she kept doing everything else the same way. The non-negotiables exercise isn't about adding more to an already-full plate. It's about deciding what comes off the plate so the non-negotiables can go on. Something has to give. And if you don't choose what gives, your body and your relationships will choose for you. That's always how it goes.

Joanna started small. She blocked Tuesday and Thursday evenings for bedtime with her kids and stopped accepting meetings after five on those days. She started running three mornings a week before the house woke up. And she told her team that she would not be available on Saturday mornings — those belonged to her family.

The sky didn't fall. Her performance didn't drop. Her boss didn't complain. In fact, nobody noticed except her. Because the person most affected by the boundaries she set wasn't anyone else. It was her. She felt different. She showed up differently. And that difference rippled through everything.

## THE REFRAME

In Chapter 2, I told Chris that good is enough — that the sentence breaks the imposter-perfectionism loop. That was about performance. This is bigger. This chapter is the whole-life version: good enough not just in your performance, but in the shape of the career and the life you're building.

Here's the thing I want every reader of this book to hear: good is enough. Not perfect. Not exceptional. Not best-in-class. Good.

I know that's a difficult message for high performers. You've been rewarded your entire career for exceeding expectations. The idea that "good enough" is a worthy target feels like settling. It's not. It's wisdom.

Perfect in one domain means broken in the others. The leader who is exceptional at work and absent at home isn't winning — they're making a trade they didn't consciously choose. The parent who is fully present at home but miserable at work isn't balanced — they're in a different kind of survival mode.

Good across the board beats exceptional in one area. And defining what "good" means — specifically, concretely, in terms that are yours and not borrowed from someone else's definition of success — is the most important career exercise most people never do.

I've had clients who did this exercise and realized they were already there. They had good. They just hadn't recognized it because they were too busy chasing more. The constant pursuit of the next thing had made them blind to the fact that what they had was already what they needed. That's a liberating realization. And it's available to anyone willing to stop and look at what they actually have instead of what they think they should want.

I've had other clients who did the exercise and realized they were nowhere close. They were excelling in one domain and neglecting the others so thoroughly that the imbalance had become their identity. For those people, the exercise was a wake-up call. Not a pleasant one. But a necessary one.

One of those clients was a man who was, by every professional measure, at the top of his game. Senior VP. Seven-figure compensation. Board visibility. The kind of career trajectory people write business school case studies about. When he did the non-negotiables exercise, he realized he was meeting all five of his work non-negotiables, two of his family non-negotiables, and none — literally none — of his personal ones.

He hadn't exercised in four months. He hadn't read a book that wasn't about business in over a year. He'd lost touch with every friend who wasn't a colleague. His entire identity was his title. And when I asked him the question — "Who are you if the job goes away tomorrow?" — he couldn't answer.

He didn't make dramatic changes. He didn't quit. He didn't take a sabbatical. He started running again. He reconnected with two old friends. He started leaving the office by six on Thursdays. Small adjustments. But each one was a reclamation of a part of himself that had been surrendered to the altar of professional achievement. And the cumulative effect was that he started to feel like a person again, not just a title.

> ***Good across the board beats exceptional in one area. Define what good means — on your terms — and then protect it.***

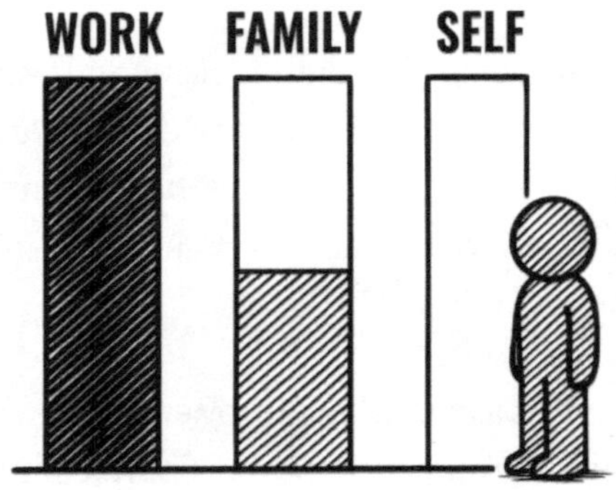


**THE BALANCE AUDIT**

*Work is full. Self is empty. That's the pattern.*

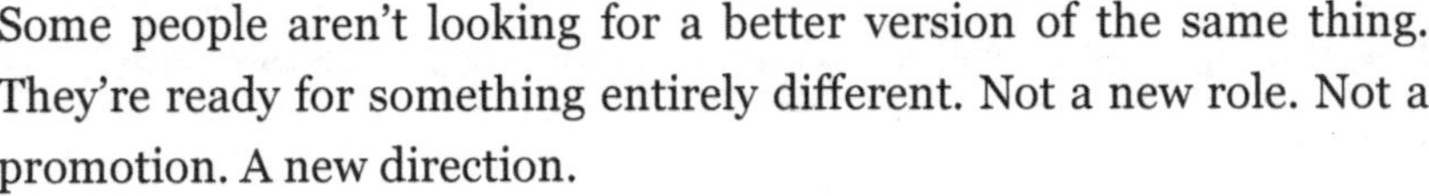

Some people aren't looking for a better version of the same thing. They're ready for something entirely different. Not a new role. Not a promotion. A new direction.

I worked with a leader who had spent 20 years in corporate life and was starting to wonder about entrepreneurship. Not in a fantasy way — in a serious, I-need-to-explore-this way. I gave her an exercise: "If you had to pick five businesses that you would enjoy or that you think you could do, what would they be? Doesn't mean you're going to do any of them. Just discover. Learn."

She came back the next session with a list that surprised both of us. Two of them were directly related to her current expertise but in completely different contexts. One was a franchise model she'd never considered. One was a business she could buy from someone who was retiring. And one was a wild card that made her light up when she talked about it.

She didn't quit her job the next day. But the exercise changed something fundamental: it reminded her that she had options. That her skills were transferable. That the corporate ladder wasn't the only structure in the world. And having that awareness — even without acting on it — made her current role feel like a choice rather than a sentence.

I give this exercise to the people I work with who are inspired by entrepreneurship, and the response is remarkably consistent. People light up. Not because they're going to become entrepreneurs tomorrow. But because the act of imagining a different life reminds them that they're not trapped. That the path they're on is one of many possible paths. That choosing to stay in a corporate role is a valid choice — but it should be a choice, not a default they never examined.

The exercise is also revealing because of what makes the list. When someone who has spent 20 years in supply chain management puts "woodworking studio" on their five businesses list, that tells you something about what's missing in their current life. Not that they should open a woodworking studio. But that creativity, working with their hands, making tangible things — those needs exist and they're not being met. That's data. And it can be addressed without a career change, if the person is willing to make room for it.

## THE FRAMEWORK

This is the chapter I almost didn't write the tools for — because these aren't about performance or visibility or managing anyone else. They're about you. What does good look like — across work, family, and self — and what would it take to actually protect it? I've given these exercises to 100s of clients. The ones who do them tend to stop chasing.

***Tool #1: The Non-Negotiables Exercise.*** This is the tool I wish someone had given me 20 years ago. I spent the first half of my career defining success by other people's metrics and wondering why achievement felt hollow. The non-negotiables exercise is what finally broke that cycle — for me and for 100s of clients since. In three columns — Work, Family, Self — write three to five non-negotiables for each. Not goals. Not wishes. Non-negotiables. The things that must be true for you to consider your life good. Then audit your current reality against the list. Where are the gaps? Those gaps are your priority, not whatever your company's development plan says.

***Tool #2: The Calendar Audit.*** Your calendar doesn't lie. Look at the last two weeks and categorize every block: was it work, family, or self? Then compare the ratio to what you said your non-negotiables were. The gap between your stated priorities and your calendar is the gap between who you say you are and who you're actually being. Most people find this exercise uncomfortable. That discomfort is the point.

| NON-NEGOTIABLES | | CURRENT STATE | |
|---|---|---|---|
| = | = | = | = |
| = | = | X | X |
| = | = | X | |
| = | = | | |
| = | = | | |

**THE NON-NEGOTIABLES GRID**

*What does good look like - for you?*

**Tool #3: The Five Businesses Exercise.** This isn't for everyone. But for the clients who do it, the effect is consistently liberating. Even if you have no intention of leaving your career, sit down and brainstorm five businesses you could realistically start or buy. Not fantasy. Not "win the lottery" scenarios. Real paths that use your actual skills, relationships, and experience.

Here's how to get started. Ask yourself three questions: What do people already come to me for — even informally? What problems do I solve that someone would pay for? And what industry or domain do I know well enough to see gaps that others miss?

Write down five options. They might be consulting practices, franchises, advisory roles, a product idea, a firm you could acquire. They don't need to be good ideas. They need to be possible ideas. The point isn't to build a business plan. The point is to break the assumption that your current path is the only path.

I had a client — a VP of operations at a logistics company — who did this exercise expecting it to be hypothetical. Within 30 minutes she had five legitimate options on paper, three of which she'd never considered. She didn't leave her job. But she stopped treating it like the only thing keeping her life together. And that shift — from trapped to choosing — changed how she showed up the next Monday morning.

The exercise is liberating even if you never act on a single one.

***Tool #4: The "What Does Good Look Like?" Conversation.*** Have this conversation with your partner, your closest friend, or your coach. Not "What does great look like?" Not "What's the dream?" Just: What does good look like? A good week. A good month. A good year. Define it in concrete, specific terms. Then notice how much of it you already have. And how much you've been too busy chasing "great" to notice.

## THE EXPERIMENT

Do the non-negotiables exercise this week. All three columns. Be honest. Then look at your calendar from the past two weeks and grade yourself. Where are you meeting your non-negotiables? Where are you falling short? And what's one thing you could change in the next seven days to close one gap?

Then have the "what does good look like?" conversation with someone who knows you well. Not your boss. Someone who sees you as a whole person, not just a professional. Listen to what they say. It will probably be different from what you expected. And it will probably be more useful than anything in your development plan.

## THE MIRROR

- What are you actually chasing? Can you name it specifically? Or is the pursuit itself the thing you're addicted to?

- What does "good enough" look like in work, family, and self? Write it down. Look at it. How much of it do you already have that you're not seeing?

- If you achieved everything on your professional wish list tomorrow, what would you do with the space that opened up? If you don't have an answer, that's worth exploring.

- Look at your calendar from the last two weeks. Does it reflect the non-negotiables you say you have? If the calendar and the list don't match, the calendar is telling the truth.

- Whose definition of success are you chasing? Be specific. If it's yours, you should be able to say so clearly. If it belongs to someone else, that's worth knowing.

- If nobody was keeping score — no performance review, no promotion path, no external validation — what would you do differently? That gap is the most important thing on this page.

## CLOSING

# THE VIEW FROM HERE

*What I've learned from sitting across from more than a thousand leaders*

---

I want to tell you what happens at the end of a coaching engagement.

It's usually our last session. Sometimes the person knows it's the last one. Sometimes they don't. But there's a quality to those final conversations that's different from everything that came before. The urgency is gone. The specific problems have either been resolved or accepted. And what's left is something simpler and more important: a person who sees themselves more clearly than they did six months ago.

Not a different person. The same person, with fewer blind spots.

That's what I hope this book has done for you. Not transformed you. Not given you a new personality or a new set of skills that feel foreign. Just held up a mirror — in enough different lights, at enough different angles — that you can see yourself a little more accurately than you could before.

Because here's what I've learned from sitting across from all those individuals: the answers were always there. In every single case. The person who couldn't figure out how to delegate? She knew how. She just couldn't tolerate watching someone else do it differently. The executive who was avoiding a difficult conversation? He knew exactly what needed to be said. He was just afraid of what saying it would cost. The leader who felt like an imposter? She had a drawer full of evidence that she belonged. She'd just never opened it.

Nobody I've ever coached needed me to give them the answer. They needed me to sit with them while they found it. That's the most humbling part of this work — and the most hopeful. Because it means the capability isn't something you have to go acquire. It's something you already have that's waiting to be uncovered.

If I had to distill everything in these 12 chapters into a handful of truths, they would be these:

The work that got you here won't get you there. Every promotion is an expert-to-beginner transition. Stop clinging to the old altitude. The new one is uncomfortable. That's the point.

Your identity needs to catch up with your role. Most of what feels like imposter syndrome is just identity lag. You're using an outdated map. Update it.

The stories you're telling yourself are running the show. Separate facts from assumptions from emotions. Challenge the assumptions. Name the emotions.

Stop being the expert. Start being the leader. Let go of solving, fixing, and rescuing. Build people who can do those things without you.

Have the conversation. The one you've been avoiding. This week. It's easier than you think.

Make yourself visible. Not political. Visible. Your work doesn't speak for itself. It needs a narrator.

Protect your energy like it's a finite resource. Because it is. Burnout doesn't announce itself. It normalizes itself.

Define good on your own terms. Good across work, family, and self beats exceptional in any one domain. And most people already have more of it than they realize.

I started this book by saying it came from a pattern. Let me end with a different one.

At the end of almost every coaching engagement, the person says some version of the same thing: "You asked the questions I didn't know I needed to be asked."

That's the whole job. Not giving answers. Asking the right questions and then creating the space for someone to sit with the discomfort long enough to find their own answer.

This book has been my attempt to do that at scale. Imperfect, necessarily incomplete, but honest. Every story, every framework, every mirror question — it all comes from real experience. My own 30 years of leading, followed by 7 years of sitting across from leaders who were brave enough to look at themselves clearly and do the work to change. The frameworks weren't borrowed from textbooks. They were built in the field, tested on myself first, and then refined through thousands of conversations until they worked.

You picked up this book for a reason. Something in the title or the description or the table of contents resonated. Trust that instinct.

I think about my clients often. Not the problems we solved — the moments when something shifted. The VP who realized her avoidance was visible to everyone except her. The director who asked "What would you do if I weren't here?" for the first time and watched his team surprise him. The GM who finally defined "good" on his own terms and discovered he already had most of it. Those moments — quiet, private, sometimes uncomfortable — are where leadership actually develops.

You've had moments like that reading this book. The question is whether you'll do anything with them.

Go back to the chapter that hit the hardest. Reread The Mirror section. Answer the questions you skipped. Do the experiment. Have the conversation.

The capability is already there. It always was. You just needed someone to ask.

Find the right altitude.

Lead from there.

And define good on your own terms.

That's the game. Now go play it.

# THE INFLUENCE FRAMEWORK

*The model underneath this book. Seven dimensions of how leaders build the ability to move people toward outcomes without relying on authority alone.*

Influence is a practice, not a personality trait. It's the ability to move people toward an outcome when you don't have the authority to simply make it happen. The Influence Framework maps how that ability actually gets built — not as a ladder you climb, but as a web of interconnected dimensions that reinforce or undermine each other.

The framework operates inside a container: the tension between **Organizational Preferences** (their priorities, their language, how decisions get made, what the organization values) and **Personal Identity** (your values, your strengths, your experience, your style). Influence lives at the intersection. Leaders stall when they over-index on one side: either conforming so completely they lose themselves, or holding so tightly to their own style they can't read the room.

## THE SEVEN DIMENSIONS

**Self-Management** — How you show up in every situation, not just the easy ones. Chapters 1, 2, 3, 11.

**Executive Presence** — How others perceive you and everything you do. Chapter 8.

**Results** — What you and your team get done. The proof that earns you the right to be heard. Chapters 1, 4, 6.

**Communication** — The message people actually receive, not what you intend. Chapters 5, 8.

**Credibility** — What people think of when they think of you. Chapters 3, 4.

**Relationships** — Connections in constant motion. The trust you build, maintain, and sometimes let go of. Chapters 5, 6, 7.

**Visibility** — What people actually see and know about you, and having advocates who speak for you when you're not in the room. Chapters 7, 9.

Every chapter in this book touches multiple dimensions. The altitude problem is a Self-Management and Results question. The dentist trap is Credibility and Visibility. The conversations you're avoiding sit at the intersection of Communication and Relationships. The framework isn't separate from the book — it's the architecture underneath it.

*For a deeper exploration of the framework — including the 50-trait Executive Presence diagnostic and the full seven-dimension model — visit therightaltitudebook.com.*

# ABOUT THE AUTHOR

**Don Eash** spent three decades leading teams and organizations before he ever coached anyone. He operated below his altitude. He avoided difficult conversations. He created dependencies instead of independence. He burned out more than once.

The seven years and six thousand hours he has spent coaching other leaders didn't come from a textbook. They came from 30 years of making the same mistakes his clients make — and eventually learning how to do it differently.

Don holds the Master Certified Coach (MCC) and Advanced Certification in Team Coaching (ACTC) credentials from the International Coaching Federation. Before coaching, he served as a senior technology and operations executive at Disney, Universal Orlando Resort, Wellspan Health, Gateway Ticketing Systems, and other organizations. He has coached professionals across Google, Meta, LinkedIn, AT&T, and dozens of other organizations.

The philosophy he brings to coaching — and to this book — is simple: push with care. He will challenge you, ask the question you've been avoiding, and point out the pattern you're not seeing. But he does it because he cares about where you're going, not because he enjoys watching people squirm.

Don lives in Gettysburg, Pennsylvania.

# RECOMMENDED READING

*These are books that have shaped how I think about leadership, coaching, and the challenges in these pages. They're not prerequisites — but if this book resonated with you, these will too.*

1. **What Got You Here Won't Get You There** by Marshall Goldsmith — The original altitude problem, framed as behavioral habits. If Chapter 1 hit home, start here.

2. **The Coaching Habit** by Michael Bungay Stanier — Seven questions that change how you lead conversations. The best practical guide to coaching-style leadership I've found.

3. **Fierce Conversations** by Susan Scott — If Chapter 5 made you uncomfortable, this book goes deeper into the art of saying the hard thing. Required reading for anyone who avoids conflict.

4. **Multipliers** by Liz Wiseman — The research behind Chapter 6. Why the best leaders make everyone around them smarter, and what the rest of us do instead.

5. **The First 90 Days** by Michael Watkins – The transition playbook. Especially relevant to Chapters 1, 2, and 8. Essential for anyone starting a new role.

6. **Dare to Lead** by Brené Brown – Vulnerability as a leadership practice, not a weakness. Complements the Mirror sections throughout this book.

7. **Radical Candor** by Kim Scott – The framework for caring personally while challenging directly. Pairs naturally with Chapters 5 and 6.

8. **Quiet** by Susan Cain – For everyone who read Chapter 8 and thought, "But I'm an introvert." Presence isn't about volume. This book proves it.

9. **Essentialism** by Greg McKeown – The disciplined pursuit of less. If Chapters 11 and 12 resonated, this is the operating system behind them.

10. **Turn the Ship Around!** by L. David Marquet – A submarine commander who stopped giving orders and started developing leaders. The military version of Chapter 6, and one of the best leadership books ever written.

# INDEX OF TOOLS

## Symbols



## A



## B



## C

## E



## F



## G



## I



## L



## M



## N



## O

## P



## R



## S



## T



## V



## W

www.ingramcontent.com/pod-product-compliance
Lightning Source LLC
LaVergne TN
LVHW091203150826
845672LV00005B/1224

* 9 7 9 8 9 9 4 9 4 8 7 0 5 *